オールカラー

英語で紹介する日本

JAPAN

Introduced in
English & Japanese

桑原功次 ＝著
Kuwabara Koji

bunraku

kagura

han-nya

sumoo

kendoo

manekineko

shikki

ナツメ社

Introduction

This book will open your eyes. You'll be surprised to find two important things about the Japanese. Firstly, the Japanese are thinking and doing the same things as your neighbors. Secondly, at the same time, they are thinking and doing things quite differently than your neighbors. They may sometimes seem like alien beings to you, but be assured they are basically gentle and kind to visitors. Have a happy encounter with the Japanese!

はじめに

　この本は、日本人の生活や文化、歴史などをわかりやすく解説し、英語を学んでいるみなさんと日本に興味を持っている外国の方々のお役に立つようにまとめられたものです。この本を使って、私たちの持っているすばらしい文化を、外国の人たちに説明してあげてください。

著　者

CONTENTS

英語で紹介する日本　JAPAN

も・く・じ

PART1 Welcome to Japan
日本へようこそ

PART2 Communication
コミュニケーション

PART 3 Sightseeing
観光

PART 4 History & Culture
歴史と文化

PART5 Food & Cooking
食べ物と料理

PART 6 Japanese Life Style
日本のライフスタイル

● 本書では、日本語の読みをローマ字で表記してあります。その際、「おはよう」は "Ohayoo" と、実際に口に出して言うときの音に近くなるようにしてあります。同様に「ありがとう」は "arigatoo" です。また、「を」は "wo" と表記してあります。

● ローマ字による日本語の表記には、外国の方が読みやすいように、必要に応じて－（ハイフン）を入れてあります。

日本の地図

nihon no chizu

31 Hiroshima
広島

32 Okayama
岡山

33 Tottori
鳥取

34 Shimane
島根

35 Yamaguchi
山口

8 Niigata
新潟

9 Toyama
富山

10 Ishikawa
石川

11 Hukui
福井

12 Gihu
岐阜

13 Nagano
長野

14 Yamanashi
山梨

15 Aichi
愛知

16 Shizuoka
静岡

40 Hukuoka
福岡

41 Saga
佐賀

42 Nagasaki
長崎

43 Ohita
大分

44 Kumamoto
熊本

45 Miyazaki
宮崎

46 Kagoshima
鹿児島

47 Okinawa
沖縄

36 Tokushima
徳島

37 Ehime
愛媛

38 Kagawa
香川

39 Kohchi
高知

27 Hyogo
兵庫

24 Osaka
大阪

28 Shiga
滋賀

25 Kyoto
京都

29 Mie
三重

26 Nara
奈良

30 Wakayama
和歌山

The population of Japan is 126 million and over 10% of it lives in Tokyo. （→和訳）

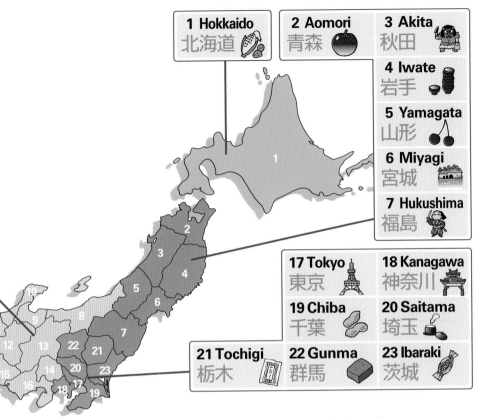

1 Hokkaido 北海道	2 Aomori 青森	3 Akita 秋田
	4 Iwate 岩手	
	5 Yamagata 山形	
	6 Miyagi 宮城	
	7 Hukushima 福島	

17 Tokyo 東京	18 Kanagawa 神奈川
19 Chiba 千葉	20 Saitama 埼玉
21 Tochigi 栃木	22 Gunma 群馬	23 Ibaraki 茨城

The length of Japanese Archipelago is 2000㎞(1250miles).
●日本列島の長さは、2000㎞（1250マイル）です。

Did you know?(知ってましたか？)

There are many dialects in Japan,for example,"Thank you." in Tokyo is "Arigatoo" but in Osaka they say "Ookini". Also "a fool" in Tokyo is "Baka", but "Aho" in Osaka.

●日本には、多くの方言があります。たとえば、東京では“ありがとう”と言いますが、大阪では“おおきに”と言います。また、東京では“バカ”と言いますが、大阪では“アホ”です。

季節・月・祝日
kisetsu, tsuki, shukujitsu

Seasons & Months（季節と月）

春
spring
はる
haru

March
3月
san-gatsu

April
4月
shi-gatsu

May
5月
go-gatsu

夏
summer
なつ
natsu

June
6月
roku-gatsu

July
7月
shichi-gatsu

August
8月
hachi-gatsu

midsummer
真夏
manatsu

秋
fall/autumn
あき
aki

September
9月
ku-gatsu

October
10月
juu-gatsu

late fall
晩秋
banshuu

冬
winter
ふゆ
huyu

November
11月
juuichi-gatsu

December
12月
juuni-gatsu

January
1月
ichi-gatsu

February
2月
ni-gatsu

early winter
初冬
shotoo

I like spring best.
私は春がいちばん好きです。
watashi wa haru ga ichiban suki desu

We change our dress for the season in June and in October. (→和訳)

National Holidays (祝日)

What day is it?
今日は何の日ですか？
kyoo wa nan-no hi desuka

January 1 / 1月1日	**New Year's day** 元旦 gantan
second monday of January / 1月第2月曜日	**Coming-of-age Day** 成人の日 seijin no hi
February 11 / 2月11日	**National Founding day** 建国記念の日 kenkoku kinen no hi
March 20(21) / 3月20(21)日	**Vernal Equinox Day** 春分の日 shunbun no hi
April 29 / 4月29日	**Greenery Day** みどりの日 midori no hi
May 3 / 5月3日	**Constitution Memorial Day** 憲法記念日 kenpoo kinenbi
May 5 / 5月5日	**Children's Day/Boys' Festival** こどもの日 kodomo no hi
third monday of July / 7月第3月曜日	**Marine Day** 海の日 umi no hi
third monday of September / 9月第3月曜日	**Respect-for-the-Aged day** 敬老の日 keiroo no hi
September 23 / 9月23日	**Autumnal Equinox Day** 秋分の日 shuubun no hi
second monday of October / 10月第2月曜日	**Sport Day** 体育の日 taiiku no hi
November 3 / 11月3日	**Culture Day** 文化の日 bunka no hi
November 23 / 11月23日	**Labor Thanksgiving Day** 勤労感謝の日 kinroo kansha no hi
December 23 / 12月23日	**Emperor's Birthday** 天皇誕生日 ten-noo tanjoobi

6月と10月に、季節に合わせて衣（ころも）替えをする。

数字とお金
suuji to okane

Numbers（数字）

one 一 ichi	two 二 ni	three 三 san	four 四 shi/yon	five 五 go	six 六 roku	seven 七 shichi/nana
eight 八 hachi	nine 九 kyuu/ku	ten 十 juu	eleven 十一 juu-ichi	twelve 十二 juu-ni	thirteen 十三 juu-san	fourteen 十四 juu-shi
fifteen 十五 juu-go	sixteen 十六 juu-roku	seventeen 十七 juu-shichi juu-nana	eighteen 十八 juu-hachi	nineteen 十九 juu-kyuu juu-ku	twenty 二十 nijuu	twenty-three 二十三 nijuu-san
thirty 三十 sanjuu	forty-three 四十三 yonjuu-san	fifty 五十 gojuu	sixty-eight 六十八 rokujuu-hachi	eighty-seven 八十七 hachijuu-nana	ninety 九十 kyuujuu	hundred 百 hyaku

thousand 千 sen	ten thousand 万 man	hundred thousand 十万 juu-man

Counting（モノを数えるとき）

1 hitotsu
2 futatsu
3 mittsu
4 yottsu
5 itsutsu
6 muttsu
7 nanatsu
8 yattsu
9 kokonotsu
10 too

10まで数えるよ
Let's count until ten.

In Japanese, four and nine are unlucky numbers. 4 (shi) means "death" and 9 (ku) means

Japanese currency（日本のお金）

一円
ichi en
¥1

— sapling
若木

五円
go en
¥5

— rice stalk
稲

十円
juu en
¥10

The Byoodooin Temple in Kyoto
京都の平等院鳳凰堂

— chrysanthemum
菊

五十円
gojuu en
¥50

百円
hyaku en
¥100

五百円
gohyaku en
¥500

千円
sen en
¥1,000

Hideyo Noguchi : famous doctor
野口英世：有名な医者

二千円
nisen en
¥2,000

Shuri Castle of Okinawa
沖縄の首里城

五千円
go-sen en
¥5,000

Ichiyou Higuchi : writer,poetess
樋口一葉：作家、詩人

一万円
ichiman en
¥10,000

Yukichi Hukuzawa : enlightenment thinker
福沢諭吉：啓蒙思想家

Did you know?（知ってましたか?）

When counting normally, one needs to specify the unit（to the cardinal number）in conjunction with the number of items.
For example,

	paper（紙）	animal（動物）	squid（イカ）	drawer（タンス）
Number＋ （数字＋）	枚 mai 	匹 hiki	杯 hai	竿 sao

●もっと正式にものを数える場合は、基本の数字のうしろにいろいろな単位をつけて数えます。

時間の流れ
jikan no nagare

Day & Night (昼と夜)

in the day time
昼間
hiruma

in the morning
朝／午前中
asa/gozenchuu

in the afternoon
午後
gogo

in the evening
夕方
yuugata

dawn
夜明け
yoake

at midnight
真夜中
mayonaka

at night
夜
yoru

Day (日にち)

yesterday
きのう
kinoo

tomorrow
明日
ashita/asu

5 6 7 8 9

the day before yesterday
おととい
ototoi

today
今日
kyoo

the day after tomorrow
あさって
asatte

Week, Month, Year (週・月・年)

week 週 shuu	last week 先週 senshuu	this week 今週 konshuu	next week 来週 raishuu
month 月 tsuki/getsu	last month 先月 sengetsu	this month 今月 kongetsu	next month 来月 raigetsu
year 年 nen/toshi	last year 去年 kyonen	this year 今年 kotoshi	next year 来年 rainen

after two weeks
2週間後
ni-shuukan go

three weeks ago
3週間前
san-shuukan mae

Days (曜日)

What day is it?
今日は何曜日ですか？
kyoo wa nan-yoobi desuka

Monday
月曜日
getsu-yoobi

Wednesday
水曜日
sui-yoobi

Friday
金曜日
kin-yoobi

Sunday
日曜日
nichi-yoobi

Tuesday
火曜日
ka-yoobi

Thursday
木曜日
moku-yoobi

Saturday
土曜日
do-yoobi

時間と日付
jikan to hizuke

Welcome to Japan

What time is it now?
今、何時ですか？
ima nanji desuka

Time (時間)

It's seven.
7時です。
shichi-ji desu

I get up at 7.
7時に起きます。
shichi-ji ni okimasu

It's 7:30.
7時30分です。
shichi-ji sanjuppun desu

I have breakfast at 7:30.
7時30分に朝食を食べます。
shichi-ji sanjuppun ni chooshoku wo tabemasu

It's 8:17.
8時17分です。
hachi-ji juunanahun desu

I leave my house at 8.
8時に家を出ます。
hachi-ji ni ie wo demasu

It's 8:20.
8時20分です。
hachi-ji nijuppun desu

I take the subway at 8:20.
8時20分に地下鉄に乗ります。
hachi-ji nijuppun ni chikatetsu ni norimasu

It's 9.
9時です。
ku-ji desu

I arrive at the office at 9.
9時に会社に着きます。
ku-ji ni kaisha ni tsukimasu

It's noon.
12時（正午）です。
juuni-ji (shoogo) desu

I have lunch at noon.
12時（正午）に昼食を食べます。
juuni-ji (shoogo) ni chuushoku wo tabemasu

Date（日付）

the first

1日
tsuitachi

the second

2日
hutsuka

the third

3日
mikka

the fourth

4日
yokka

the fifth
5日
itsuka

the twentieth

20日 20
hatsuka

What's the date?
今日は何日ですか？
kyoo wa nan-nichi desuka

the sixth

6日
muika

the fourteenth

14日
juu-yokka

the tenth

10日
tooka

the ninth

9日
kokonoka

the eighth

8日
yooka

the seventh

7日
nanoka

Other Expressions（そのほかの表現）

It's about ten.
10時ごろです。
juu-ji goro desu

It's almost five.
もうすぐ5時です。
moosugu go-ji desu

punctual
時間に正確
jikan ni seikaku

not punctual
時間にだらしない
jikan ni darashinai

You came home after midnight again!
また午前様なのね！
mata gozensama nanone

It's 5.
5時です。
go-ji desu

I finish working at 5.
5時に仕事が終わります。
go-ji ni shigoto ga owarimasu

It's 7:25.
7時25分です。
shichi-ji nijuugohun desu

I come home at 7:25.
7時25分に帰宅します。
shichi-ji nijuugohun ni kitaku shimasu

人の呼び方
hito no yobikata

Calling (人の呼び方)

I
私
watashi

you
あなた／君
anata/kimi

he
彼
kare

they
彼ら
karera

she
彼女
kanojo

they
彼女たち
kanojo tachi

that person
あの人
ano hito

this person
この人
kono hito

Informal calling (くだけた表現)

I
ぼく
boku

you
おまえ
omae

this fellow
こいつ
koitsu

these fellows
こいつら
koitsura

you
おまえたち／おまえら
omaetachi/omaera

that fellow
あいつ
aitsu

we
ぼくたち／ぼくら
bokutachi/bokura

those fellows
あいつら
aitsura

Calling（呼びかけ）

Say!/Excuse me!
あの〜／すみません／ちょっと
anoo　　　sumimasen　　chotto

"Sumimasen" is a very useful expression. Sumimasen＝(we also pronounce) "Suimasen".
●「すみません」は便利な表現です。「すみません」と「すいません」は同じ意味です。

A call from far away
（遠くの人を呼ぶとき）

Sumimase〜n !

Sumimasen =I'm sorry.
ごめんなさい。

Suimasen = I don't smoke.
（タバコは）吸いません。

Did you know?（知ってましたか?）

In America and Europe, when beckoning a person, it is done with the hand, palm up with a raking motion. But in Japan, it is done with the hand palm down with a raking motion. We sometimes use the American or European hand gesture to call dogs or cats.

●欧米では、人を呼ぶときは手のひらを上に向けて呼びますが、日本では手のひらを下に向けて呼びます。日本では欧米式のやり方を犬や猫に対してやることがあります。

日本人は、自分のへその緒を保存する人が多い。 **19**

あいさつ
aisatsu

You have to stop and bow when you make a formal greetings.
- ●ていねいなあいさつでは、立ち止まって頭を下げます。
When we make informal greetings, we sometimes raise up our dominant hand instead of bowing.
- ●くだけたあいさつでは、頭を下げずに利き手をあげる人がいます。

Morning
朝
asa

Good morning.
- ●おはようございます。
ohayoo gozaimasu
- ●おはよう。
ohayoo

Afternoon
午後
gogo

Good afternoon.
- ●こんにちは。
kon-nichiwa
- ●こんちは。
konchiwa

Night
夜
yoru

Good night.
- ●おやすみなさい。
oyasuminasai
- ●おやすみ。
oyasumi

Farewell Greetings
別れのあいさつ
wakare no aisatsu

- ●**Good-bye.**
さよなら。
sayonara
- ●**See you.**
それじゃ。
sorejaa
- ●**Take care.**
じゃあね。
jaane

Good morning in Japanese is "Ohayoo gozaimasu". It means "We meet early in the morning".

Formal

How are you?
お元気ですか？
ogenki desuka

I'm fine thank you.
はい、おかげさまで。
hai okagesamade

Are you busy?
おいそがしいですか？
oisogashii desuka

Well,not too bad.
まあまあです。
maamaa desu

Informal

What's up?
元気？
genki

Not bad.
元気。
genki

Busy?
いそがしい？
isogashii

So-so.
まあまあ。
maamaa

Other greetings（そのほかのあいさつ）

I'm leaving!
行ってきます！
itte kimasu

Have a nice day!
行ってらっしゃい！
itte rasshai

I'm home!
ただいま！
tadaima

Welcome home!
お帰りなさい！
okaeri nasai

These greetings are done without hugs and kisses.
We neither hug nor kiss in front of other people.
●これらのあいさつは、抱き合ったりキスをして行われる
ものではありません。人前ではそういうことはしません。

Did you know?（知ってましたか？）

We usually ask "Where are you going?" to each other.   It is not a
strange question in Japan. The answers are not specific. For example, "chotto-soko-made. (I'm going somewhere around) is often
used. It's not for investigating your behavior.

●「どちらにお出かけですか？」などと言い
ますが、これは別にめずらしいことでは
ありません。その答えも、「ちょっとそこ
まで」などと答えます。別にあなたの行
動を詮索しているわけではありません。

紹介
shookai

Self Introduction (自己紹介)

How do you do?
はじめまして。
hajimemashite

My name is James White.
ジェームス・ホワイトです。
jeemusu-howaito desu

Nice to meet you.
よろしく
（お願いします）。
yoroshiku(onegaishimasu)

Nice to meet you, too.
こちらこそ
（よろしくお願いします）。
kochirakoso(yoroshiku onegaishimasu)

Friends (友だちを紹介)

Let me introduce my friend.
友だちを紹介します。
tomodachi wo shookai shimasu

This is Mrs. Suzuki.
こちらは鈴木さんです。
kochira wa suzuki-san desu

Names (名前を聞く)

中田れいな
naka da re i na

May I have your name?
お名前は？
onamae wa

My name is Reina Nakada.
中田れいなです。
nakada-reina desu

When you sneeze, it is said that someone is talking about you. (→和訳)

Family（家族を紹介）

This is my father.
父です。
chichi desu

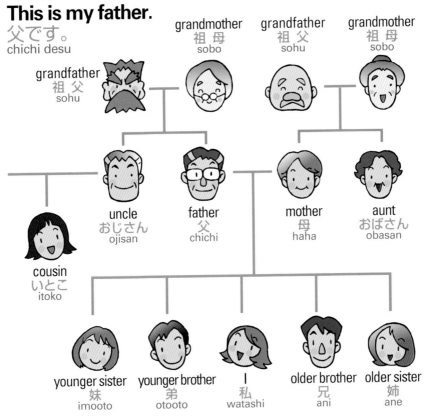

grandmother
祖母
sobo

grandfather
祖父
sohu

grandmother
祖母
sobo

grandfather
祖父
sohu

uncle
おじさん
ojisan

father
父
chichi

mother
母
haha

aunt
おばさん
obasan

cousin
いとこ
itoko

younger sister
妹
imooto

younger brother
弟
otooto

I
私
watashi

older brother
兄
ani

older sister
姉
ane

Did you know?（知ってましたか?）

After becoming friendlier, one can call a girl by putting "chan" after her first name. But not for the first time meeting.

● 親しくなったあとでは、女性を呼ぶときには名前のあとに "ちゃん" をつけて呼ぶことができますが、初対面の場合にはひんしゅくを買ってしまいます。

When Japanese introduce their family, they sometimes say "This is my dull-witted son" or " This is my silly wife" to show humility.

● 家族を紹介するとき、謙遜して "私の愚息です" "愚妻です" と言ったりします。

くしゃみが出たときは、だれかが自分のうわさをしている。

国・くに
kuni

Where are you from?
どこから来たのですか？
dokokara kitano desuka

I'm from US.
アメリカから来ました。
amerika kara kimashita

Which part of America are you from?
アメリカのどこから来たのですか？
amerika no dokokara kitano desuka

I'm from California.
カリフォルニアです。
kariforunia desu

Countries（国と地域）

USA

アメリカ
amerika

England

イギリス
igirisu

Australia

オーストラリア
oosutoraria

Brazil

ブラジル
burajiru

New Zealand

ニュージーランド
nyuujiirando

Taiwan

台湾
taiwan

Singapore

シンガポール
shingapooru

Thailand

タイ
tai

the Philippines

フィリピン
firipin

South Korea

韓国
kankoku

China

中国
chuugoku

Germany

ドイツ
doitsu

Canada

カナダ
kanada

France

フランス
huransu

Japan

日本
nippon/nihon

Did you know? (知ってましたか？)

Instead of shaking hands, the Japanese make a bow.
- ●握手のかわりに、日本人はおじ ぎをします。

At least two to three times.
- ●少なくとも2～3回。

At the department store, the clerks make a 30 degree bowing.
- ●デパートなどでは、おじぎは 30度です。

30°

Sitting straight in the tatami(straw-mat)room makes your legs numb.
- ●畳の部屋で正座をすると、足 がしびれてきます。

Put your saliva on your forehead with your index finger three times, it'll make you feel better.
- ●人さし指にツバをつけて、おで こに3回つけるとよくなると言 われています。

Sitting cross-legged is much better.
- ●あぐらをかくと、少しは楽です。

知り合う
shiriau

Questions（質問してみる）

May I have your~?
～を教えてください。
~wo oshiete kudasai

Write down your~, please.
～を書いてください。
~wo kaite kudasai

phone number
電話番号
denwa bangoo

e-mail address
Eメールアドレス
"e"meeru adoresu

cellular phone number
携帯番号
keitai bangoo

address
住所
juusho

name
名前
namae

cellular phone mail address
携帯メールアドレス
keitai meeru adoresu

schedule
予定
yotei

Where do you live?
どちらにお住まいですか？
dochira ni osumai desuka

I live in Tokyo.
東京に住んでいます。
tookyoo ni sunde imasu

Let's keep in touch.
お互いに連絡しましょう。
otagaini renraku shimashoo

Are you free this Sunday?
今度の日曜日、時間がありますか？
kondo no nichiyoobi jikan ga arimasuka

Yes, I am.
はい、あります。
hai arimasu

No, I'm not.
いいえ、ありません。
iie arimasen

"We meet only to part" in Japanese is "auwa wakare no hajime nari". (→和訳)

Answers（質問に答える）

When did you come to Japan?
いつ日本に来たのですか？
itsu nihon ni kitano desuka

Two months ago.
2か月前です。
nikagetsu mae desu

How long are you going to stay in Japan?
どのくらいいるのですか？
donokurai iruno desuka

About ten days.
10日間くらいです。
tookakan kurai desu

Is this your first time to visit Japan?
日本は初めてですか？
nihon wa hajimete desuka

It's my second time.
2回目です。
nikaime desu

What's the purpose of your visit?
なぜ日本に来たのですか？
naze nihon ni kitano desuka

---

business
仕事
shigoto

to study Japanese language
日本語の勉強をするため
nihon-go no benkyoo wo surutame

sightseeing
観光
kankoo

to study Japanese culture
日本文化の勉強をするため
nihon-bunka no benkyoo wo surutame

Did you know?（知ってましたか？）

Japanese people don't always gaze at each other's eyes while they're talking. It doesn't mean they despise them, but shows respect and politeness to them.

●日本人は、話をしている間ずっと相手の目を見て話しているわけではありません。それは、相手を軽蔑しているからではなく、相手に対する尊敬と礼儀正しさを表しているのです。

仕事
shigoto

What do you do?
仕事はなんですか？
shigoto wa nandesuka

I'm an office worker.
サラリーマンです。
sarariiman desu

Types of occupation (仕事名)

office worker
OL
ooeru

student
学生
gakusei

self-employed
自営業
jieigyoo

programmer
プログラマー
puroguramaa

government worker
公務員
koomuin

casual worker
フリーター
huriitaa

part-timer
パートタイム
paatotaimu

housewife
主婦
shuhu

engineer
エンジニア
enjinia

Licensed (免許)

licensed cook
調理師
choorishi

pharmacist
薬剤師
yakuzaishi

beautician
美容師
biyooshi

driver
運転手
untenshu

accountant
会計士
kaikeishi

doctor
医者
isha

lawyer
弁護士
bengoshi

dentist
歯医者
haisha

nurse
看護師
kangoshi

Types of business（業種）

I'm working for food business.
食べもの関係の仕事です。
tabemono kankei no shigoto desu

finance
金融
kinyuu

advertising
広告
kookoku

delivery
運送
unsoo

publishing
出版
shuppan

mass media
マスコミ
masukomi

medical
医療
iryoo

manufacturing
製造業
seizoogyoo

Did you know?（知ってましたか？）

With the increase in the aging population, followed by a decrease in the working force, a small number will be forced to support large numbers soon.

●人口の高齢化が進んでいて、働く世代の人口が減り、少しの若者が大勢の高齢者の生活を支えなくてはならない時代が、もうすぐやってきます。

仕事に熱中する人のことを"仕事人間"または"仕事中毒"という。　**29**

感情とお願い
kanjoo to onegai

Feelings（感情）

smiling face
笑 顔
egao

I'm fine.
元気です。
genki desu

I'm happy.
うれしいです。
ureshii desu

I appreciate it.
感謝しています。
kanshashite imasu

Fortune comes to a merry home.
笑う門には福来たる
waraukado niwa huku kitaru

worrying face
心配顔
shinpaigao

I feel lonely.
さびしいです。
sabishii desu

I'm sad.
悲しいです。
kanashii desu

I'm scared.
こわいです。
kowai desu

I'm worried.
心配しています。
shinpaishite imasu

No sweat!
心配ご無用!
shinpai gomuyoo

angry face
怒り顔
okorigao

I'm fed up.
うんざりです。
unzari desu

I'm angry.
怒っています。
okotte imasu

I'm disappointed.
がっかりです。
gakkari desu

I got mad!
頭にきました!
atama ni kimashita

Calm down!
ま、落ち着いて!
ma ochitsuite

Requests（お願い）

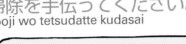

Would you do me a favor?
お願いがあります。
onegai ga arimasu

May I help you?
なんですか？
nandesuka

Please help me with the cleaning.
掃除を手伝ってください。
sooji wo tetsudatte kudasai

washing 洗濯 sentaku	**homework** 宿題 shukudai	**baggage** 荷物持ち nimotsu mochi
cooking 料理 ryoori	**calculation** 計算 keisan	**weeding** 草取り kusatori
study 勉強 benkyoo	**work** 仕事 sigoto	

No problem.
いいですよ。
iidesu-yo

I'm sorry I can't.
ごめんなさい、できません。
gomen-nasai dekimasen

Did you know?（知ってましたか？）

One puts his hands together like this when asking a favor. It's hard to say no when your friend asks you something like this.

●お願いをするときは、このように両手を合わせる人もいます。こんなふうにされると、なかなか断りにくくなります。

Onegai

おれとおわび

orei to owabi

Arigatoo gozaimasu

Thanks（お礼）

Thank you very much.
ありがとうございます。
arigatoo gozaimasu

Thank you for~.
～をありがとう。
~wo arigatoo

I appreciate it.
感謝しています。
kanshashite imasu

your kindness ご親切に *goshinsetsu ni*	your invitation ご招待 *goshoutai*	dinner ディナー *dinaa*
calling お電話 *odenwa*	everything いろいろと *iroiro-to*	the present プレゼント *purezento*

Did you know?（知ってましたか？）

The Japanese think an important thing should be wrapped properly and consider the wrapping paper as part of the important gift. It's rude to rip the wrapping paper in front of a friend. When we give money, it is always wrapped.

●日本人は、大切なものをきちんと包みます。包装紙も、大切なものの一部なのです。友だちの前で、プレゼントの包装紙を破きません。お金を渡すときも、包んで渡します。

Apologies（おわび）

I'm sorry.
ごめんなさい。
gomen-nasai

I apologize.
謝ります。
ayamarimasu

That's my fault.
私が悪いのです。
watashi ga waruino desu

Please forgive me.
許してください。
yurushite kudasai

I won't do that again.
もうしません。
moo shimasen

 I'll forgive you.
許してあげる。
yurushite ageru

To your friends（友だちなら）

Sorry.
ごめんね。
gomen-ne

That's all right.
 いいんだよ。
man/iinda-yo

 いいのよ。
woman/iino-yo

Thanks and apologies should be made with a bow.
Add "Hontooni" to the expression to tell your deeper feelings.
●感謝をしたり、謝るときは頭を下げましょう。
　表現の前に『本当に』をつけると、さらに深い意味になります。

I really thank you.
本当にありがとう。
hontoo ni arigatoo

I'm really sorry.
本当にごめんなさい。
hontoo ni gomen-nasai

PART2

理解とあいづち
rikai to aizuchi

Do you understand? (わかりますか？)

Do you speak English?
英語が話せますか？
eigo ga hanasemasuka

Do you understand Japanese?
日本語がわかりますか？
nihon-go ga wakarimasuka

 Yes.
はい。
hai

I understand.
わかりました。
wakarimashita

 A little.
少しだけ。／
ちょっとだけ。
sukoshi dake/
chotto dake

 No.
いいえ。
iie

I don't understand.
わかりません。／わかんない。
wakarimasen   wakan-nai

children, young girls（子ども、若い女の子）

Speak more slowly, please.
ゆっくり話してください。
yukkuri hanashite kudasai

Pardon?
もう一度お願いします。
mooichido onegai shimasu

I don't know.
知りません。
shirimasen

Wait a minute.
ちょっと待ってください。
chotto matte kudasai

Write it down, please.
書いてください。
kaite kudasai

Responses (あいづち)

I see.
なるほど。
naruhodo

Oh, my God!
へえ。
hee

Really?
ほんとに？
hontoni

Unbelievable!
信じられない！
shinji rarenai

For young people only (若者だけ)

You must be joking.
うっそ〜。
ussoo

Are you serious?
マジで？
maji-de

Maybe.
かもね。
kamo-ne

Mighty "Doomo!" ("どうも"の威力)

= Nice to meet you | = Thank you | = I'm sorry

= I'm afraid it's no good

= Long time no see

Mighty "Chotto!" ("ちょっと"の威力)

= I'm afraid it's no good

= Wait a minute!

= Only a little

= Hey!/Say!/Excuse me!

日本人は照れ隠しに頭をかくことがある。 **35**

東京観光地図
tookyoo kankoo chizu

We're going to Akihabara. Which line?
秋葉原に行くのですが。 何線ですか？
akihabara ni ikuno desuga   nanisen desuka

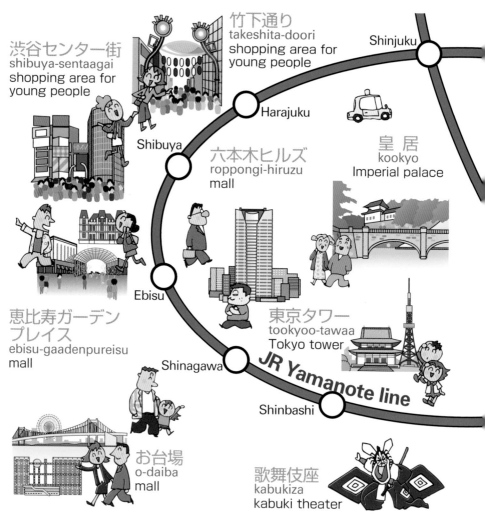

渋谷センター街
shibuya-sentaagai
shopping area for
young people

竹下通り
takeshita-doori
shopping area for
young people

Shinjuku

Harajuku

Shibuya

六本木ヒルズ
roppongi-hiruzu
mall

皇居
kookyo
Imperial palace

Ebisu

恵比寿ガーデン
プレイス
ebisu-gaadenpureisu
mall

東京タワー
tookyoo-tawaa
Tokyo tower

Shinagawa

JR Yamanote line

Shinbashi

お台場
o-daiba
mall

歌舞伎座
kabukiza
kabuki theater

Some people go under the cherry tree to secure the place for the blossom viewing party

What's the nearest station?

いちばん近い駅は？
ichiban chikai eki wa

How many minutes?

何分かかりますか？
nanpun kakarimasuka

巣鴨地蔵通り
sugamo-jizoodoori
shopping area for
old people

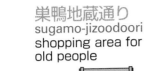

雷門
kaminarimon
gate of gods of
wind & thunder

浅草寺
sensooji
the Goddes of
mercy

Ikebukuro

Sugamo

東京ドーム
tookyoo-doomu
Tokyo dome

アメ横
ameyoko
discount shopping
street

秋葉原電気街
akihabara-denkigai
electronics town

Ueno

上野公園
ueno-kooen
ueno park

JR Chuuoo line

Akihabara

国技館
kokugikan
sumo arena

Yuurakuchoo

Tokyo

東京
ディズニーランド
tookyoo-dizuniirando
Tokyo Disneyland

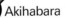

築地魚市場
tsukiji-uoichiba
fish market

PART3

電車と地下鉄①

densha to chikatetsu

Two tickets for Kyoto, please.
京都まで、2枚ください。
kyooto made nimai kudasai

They're on the ten o'clock shinkansen.
10時の新幹線でお願いします。
juuji no shinkansen de onegai shimasu

The reserved seat tickets, please.
座席指定でお願いします。
zaseki shitei de onegai shimasu

To which track should I go?
何番線に行けばいいですか？
nanbansen ni ikeba iidesuka

Super-express (新幹線)

The Shinkansen joins major cities around Japan. It runs at the maximum speed of 270km/h (169miles/h), and it's very punctual.

●新幹線は日本の主要都市を結び、最高時速270キロで走ります。とても時間に正確です。

Words about trains (関連単語)

open seat ticket
自由席
jiyuuseki

reserved seat ticket
指定席
shiteiseki

first-class
グリーン車
guriinsha

local train
普通列車
hutsuu ressha

limited express
特急
tokkyuu

express
急行
kyuukoo

semi-express
準急
junkyuu

boxed lunch
駅弁
ekiben

one-way ticket
片道切符
katamichi kippu

Japanese Railways
JR
jeeaaru

round-trip ticket
往復切符
oohuku kippu

Akihabara-!
Please change here for the Hibiya line...

They're telling you all the information you should know about the trains. You never get lost if you understand Japanese.

●駅のアナウンスは、電車についての必要な情報をすべて言っているのです。日本語がわかれば、決して迷うことはありません。

Did you know? (知ってましたか?)

Why do Japanese sleep in the train so often? They're sleeping or a little tired or meditating with their eyes closed. They know it's safe in the train and where to get off.

●なぜ、日本人は電車の中でよく寝ているのでしょうか? 彼らは寝ているか、少し疲れているか、あるいは目を閉じて瞑想しているのです。電車の中は安全で、どこで降りるかもわかっているのです。

朝のラッシュアワーには、1時間に24本の電車が来る。

電車と地下鉄②
densha to chikatetsu

How many stops to Shinbashi?
新橋はいくつ目ですか？
shinbashi wa ikutsume desuka

It's the third stop.
3つ目です。
mittsume desu

How long does it take?
どのくらいかかりますか？
donokurai kakarimasuka

It takes about fifteen minutes.
15分くらいかかります。
juugo-hun kurai kakarimasu

Is this for Shibuya?
渋谷に行きますか？
shibuya ni ikimasuka

You got a wrong train.
電車が違います。
densha ga chigaimasu

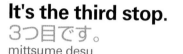

How can I get to Ginza?
どうしたら銀座に行けますか？
dooshitara ginza ni ikemasuka

Take the Ginza line.
銀座線に乗りなさい。
ginza-sen ni norinasai

Do I have to transfer?
乗り換えですか？
norikae desuka

Transfer at Shibuya.
渋谷で乗り換えなさい。
shibuya de norikaenasai

Words about trains (関連単語)

subway
地下鉄
chikatetsu

ticket gate
改札口
kaisatsu guchi

platform
ホーム
hoomu

track no.2
2番線
ni-bansen

ticket window
切符売り場
kippu uriba

ticket machine
切符販売機
kippu hanbaiki

fare
運賃
unchin

fare adjustment
清算
seisan

change
おつり
otsuri

information
案内所
an-naijo

news stand
売店
baiten

JR railway pre-paid card
イオカード
io kaado

JR-east railway pre-paid card
スイカ
suika

JR-west railway pre-paid card
イコカ
ikoka

subway pre-paid card
パスネット
pasunetto

Did you know? (知ってましたか?)

In the morning,the trains sometimes come within a minute after the last one.

● 都市部の通勤時間帯は、1分以内に次の電車が来ます。

Don't hesitate to push them out when you can't get off the train.

● 満員電車では、降りられないと思ったら、周囲の人を押し出さないと降りることができません。

その他の交通機関
sonohoka no kootsuu kikan

Bus (バス)

Where's the bus stop?
バス停はどこですか？
basutei wa doko desuka

Is this for Shinjuku?
これは新宿に行きますか？
kore wa shinjuku ni ikimasuka

Tell me when we arrive.
着いたら教えてください。
tsuitara oshiete kudasai

priority seat
優先座席
yuusen zaseki

city bus
路線バス
rosen basu

uniform fare
均一料金
kin-itsu ryookin

bus stop
バス停
basutei

Taxi (タクシー)

To Kabukiza, please.
歌舞伎座まで。
kabukiza made

Stop here, please.
ここで止めてください。
kokode tomete kudasai

How much?
いくらですか？
ikura desuka

taxi stand
タクシー乗り場
takushii noriba

traffic jam
渋滞
juutai

Airplane (飛行機)

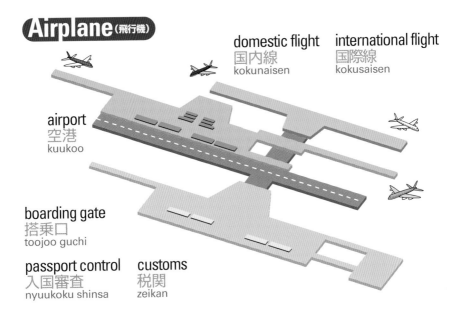

domestic flight
国内線
kokunaisen

international flight
国際線
kokusaisen

airport
空港
kuukoo

boarding gate
搭乗口
toojoo guchi

passport control
入国審査
nyuukoku shinsa

customs
税関
zeikan

Others (その他)

ferry
フェリー
ferii

sightseeing boat
遊覧船
yuuransen

railroad ferry
連絡船
renrakusen

streetcar
路面電車
romen densha

monorail
モノレール
monoreeru

Did you know?(知ってましたか?)

You don't have to give a tip to the driver even if he put your baggage in and out the trunk.

●タクシーにチップはいりません。スーツケースをトランクから出してくれたときでもいりません。

You don't have to open the door of the taxi.
It's opened automatically by the driver.

●タクシーのドアは開ける必要がありません。運転手が開けてくれます。

19 Asking the way

Sightseeing

道をたずねる
michi wo tazuneru

Where's the Japanese cake shop?
和菓子屋はどこですか？
wagashiya wa doko desuka

It's on this street.
この通りにあります。
kono toori ni arimasu

Go straight.
まっすぐ行ってください。
massugu ittekudasai

Turn left at the second corner.
2つ目の角を左に曲がってください。
hutatsume no kado wo magatte kudasai

You can't miss it.
すぐに見つかります。
suguni mitsukari masu

It's next to the ramen noodle shop.
ラーメン屋のとなりです。
raamen-ya no tonari desu

It's in front of the pharmacy.
薬局の前です。
yakkyoku no mae desu

It's on the corner.
角にあります。
kado ni arimasu

I'll take you there.
ご案内します。
goan-nai shimasu

44 South-east is the best direction to put the front door of the house. (→和訳)

Kinds of Shops（店の種類）

liquor shop
酒屋
sakaya

barber shop
床屋
tokoya

hair salon
美容室
biyooshitsu

optician's shop
眼鏡屋
meganeya

CD shop
CD屋
shiidiiya

clothing shop
洋品店
yoohinten

fruit shop
果物屋
kudamonoya

flower shop
花屋
hanaya

book shop
書店
shoten

bakery
パン屋
pan-ya

cake shop
ケーキ屋
keekiya

supermarket
スーパー
suupaa

department store
デパート（百貨店）
depaato (hyakkaten)

coffee shop
喫茶店
kissaten

hundred-yen shop
100円ショップ
hyaku-en shoppu

Landmarks（目印になるもの）

park
公園
kooen

shrine
神社
jinja

temple
寺
tera

museum
博物館
hakubutsukan

art museum
美術館
bijutsukan

Did you know?（知ってましたか?）

Japanese house numbers sometimes don't go in order. For example, next to No.1 is No.3 and No.2 is on the opposite side of the street not in front of No.1. It's not so easy to find your friend's house only with the house number.

●日本の住所の番地は、順番に並んでいないことがあります。たとえば、1の隣が3で、2は反対側の3軒向こうにあるということもあり、住所だけで友だちの家を探すのは決して簡単ではありません。

㉛ Visiting & Praying

見る・参拝する
miru sanpai suru

Temple (寺・tera)

Buddhist priests and nuns study at the temple and some Buddhist services are held there.

●お寺とは、お坊さんや尼さんが修行をしたり、さまざまな仏事を行う施設です。

There's a graveyard in the temple.

●寺の敷地内には、お墓もあります。

東大寺
toodaiji
奈良市/Nara city

©JNTO

法隆寺
houryuji
奈良県生駒郡/Ikoma,Nara

©JNTO

如来
nyorai

菩薩
bosatsu

It's believed that the smoke of the incense stick has a special power to cure disease.

Shrine (神社・jinja)

The local deities are worshipped at the local shrines.

●さまざまな神様を奉った神社が日本各地にあります。

On New Year's Day many people visit the shrine to pay their first visit of the year.

●お正月には、多くの人が神社へ初詣に行きます。

This is the way to pray at the shrine.

●お参りするときは右図のようにします。

こま犬
komainu

八坂神社
yasaka jinja
京都市/Kyoto city

鶴岡八幡宮
tsurugaoka hachimanguu
神奈川県鎌倉市/
Kamakura city,Kanagawa

©JNTO

©JNTO

Did you know? (知ってましたか?)

When you consult an oracle at the temple or the shrine, the result is as follows arranged in lucky order "dai-kichi, chuu-kichi, sho-kichi, sue-kichi and kyo". If you get "kyo", tie it up in the trees there and you'll be all right.

●神社や寺で、おみくじを引くと "大吉、中吉、小吉、末吉、凶" と書いてあります。いちばん良いのが大吉で、悪いのが凶です。凶が出たら、境内の木に結んでしまえば大丈夫です。

PART3

Famous Temples & Shrines (有名な寺と神社)

金閣寺（鹿苑寺）
kinkakuji(rokuonji)
京都市/Kyoto city

銀閣寺（慈照寺）
ginkakuji(jishooji)
京都市/Kyoto city

清水寺
kiyomizudera
京都市/Kyoto city

©JNTO

東大寺
toodaiji
奈良市/Nara city

薬師寺
yakushiji
奈良市/Nara city

三十三間堂
sanjuu-sangendoo
京都市/Kyoto city

Famous Castles (有名な城)

名古屋城
nagoyajoo
愛知県名古屋市/
Nagoya city,Aichi

大阪城
oosakajoo
大阪市/Osaka city

姫路城
himejijoo
兵庫県姫路市/
Himeji city,Hyoogo

48 Before praying at the shrine, we have to wash our hands and rinse out our mouths. (→和訳)

龍安寺
ryooanji
京都市/Kyoto city
©JNTO

仁和寺
nin-naji
京都市/Kyoto city
©JNTO

平安神宮
heian jinguu
京都市/Kyoto city
©JNTO

春日大社
kasugataisha
奈良市/Nara city
©JNTO

厳島神社
itsukushima jinja
広島県宮島町/
Miyajima,Hiroshima
©JNTO

日光東照宮
nikkoo tooshooguu
栃木県日光市/
Nikko city,Tochigi
©JNTO

Did you know? (知ってましたか?)

Mt. Fuji is the highest mountain in Japan and famous for its beautiful shape. It is said to be Japanese people's spiritual home.

●富士山は日本一高い山で、その美しさは有名です。日本人の心のふるさととともいえる存在です。

神社に参拝する前には、手を洗い、口をすすいで身を清める。 **49**

日本の祭り

nihon no matsuri

What's this festival?
これは何のお祭りですか？
kore wa nan-no omatsuri desuka

When is this festival?
このお祭りは、
いつやっていますか？
kono omatsuri wa itsu yatte imasuka

That sounds exciting.
おもしろそうだ。
omoshiro sooda

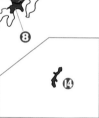

Famous festivals（有名な祭り）

❶ 雪祭り
yuki matsuri
snow festival

北海道・2月
Hokkaidoo・Feb.

❷ ねぶた祭り
nebuta matsuri
huge lantern
float

青森県・8月
Aomori・Aug.

❸ なまはげ
namahage
men wearing
demon mask
visit the house

秋田県・2月
Akita・Feb.

❹ 竿燈
kantoo
bamboo pole
with many
lanterns

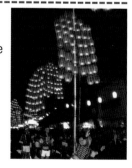

秋田県・8月
Akita・Aug.

❺ 七夕祭り
tanabata matsuri
star festival

宮城県・8月
Miyagi・Aug.

©JNTO

❻ 花笠祭り
hanagasa matsuri
dancers
wearing
flower hats

山形県・8月
Yamagata・Aug.

❼ 三社祭
sanja matsuri
gigantic
portable
shrine

東京都・5月
Tokyo・May

©JNTO

❽ 流鏑馬
yabusame
shooting
arrows on
horseback

神奈川県・9月
Kanagawa・Sep.

©JNTO

❾ 葵祭
aoi matsuri
dressed in
costumes of
Heian period

京都府・5月
Kyoto・May

観覧席（京都御苑・下鴨神社）1席2,000円

❿ 祇園祭
gion matsuri
parade of
decorated
floats

京都府・7月
Kyoto・July

観覧席（御池通）1席3,100円

⓫ 阿波踊り
awaodori
dancing
parade with
simple duple
time

徳島県・8月
Tokushima・Aug.

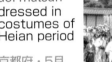

⓬ どんたく
dontaku
parade of
beautifully
ornamented
floats

福岡県・5月
Hukuoka・May

©JNTO

⓭ おくんち
okunchi
dancing in a
huge float of
a snake

長崎県・10月
Nagasaki・Oct.

©JNTO

⓮ 沖縄全島エイサー祭り
okinawa zentoo
eisaa matsuri
dancing and
musical per-
formance

沖縄県・9月
Okinawa・Sep.

PART3

22 Staying at "Ryokan"

旅館に泊まる
ryokan ni tomaru

Ryokan people（旅館の人々）

女将
okami
landlady

番頭
bantoo
staff manager

仲居
nakai
maid

板前
itamae
chef

Ryokan room（部屋の様子）

❶ cushion
座布団
zabuton

❷ legless chair
座いす
zaisu

❸ safe
金庫
kinko

❹ informal cotton kimono
浴衣
yukata

The maid in charge comes to greet and serve tea.
●仲居さんが部屋に来て、あいさつをしてお茶を入れてくれます。

Where's the open-air bath?

露天風呂はどこですか？

rotenburo wa doko desuka

What time is the dinner?

夕食は何時ですか？

yuushoku wa nanji desuka

Words (関連単語)

large public bath
大浴場
daiyokujoo

family bath
家族風呂
kazokuburo

open-air bath
露天風呂
rotenburo

mixed-bathing
混浴
kon-yoku

bath in the morning
朝風呂
asaburo

banquet
宴会
enkai

banquet hall
宴会場
enkaijoo

spree
ドンチャン騒ぎ
donchan sawagi

geisha
芸者
geisha

karaoke
カラオケ
karaoke

Did you know? (知ってましたか?)

The futons are spread out when the guests are out of the room by the ryokan staff.

●布団は、お客さんが部屋にいないときに従業員が敷いてくれます。

Take a bath at least an hour later the meals and exercise.

●温泉に入るのは、食事、運動のあと約1時間以上たってから。

A long bath sometimes causes dehydration and dizziness.

●長く入りすぎると、脱水症状、めまい、ほてりなどを起こすので注意。

日本の温泉
nihon no onsen

What is this hot spring good for?
この温泉は何に効きますか？
kono onsen wa nani ni kikimasuka

What's the effect?
効能は何ですか？
koonoo wa nandesuka

It's good for chills.
冷え症によく効きます。
hieshoo ni yoku kikimasu

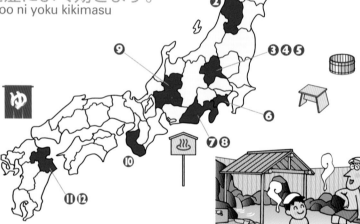

Effects（効能）

肩 stiff back
肩こり
katakori

リ rheumatism
リュウマチ
ryuumachi

吹 pimples
吹き出物
hukidemono

皮 skin ailments
皮膚病
hihubyoo

疲 fatigue
疲労
hiroo

傷 cuts/burns
切り傷／やけど
kirikizu/yakedo

冷 chills
冷え症
hieshoo

婦 chronic feminine ailments
慢性婦人病
mansei hujinbyoo

An egg boiled in the spa is a Japanese favorite. （→和訳）

Famous hot springs & Effects（有名な温泉地と効能）

❶ 登別温泉
noboribetsu onsen

北海道　Hokkaidoo

❷ 蔵王温泉
zaoo onsen

山形県　Yamagata

❸ 水上温泉
minakami onsen

群馬県　Gunma

❹ 草津温泉
kusatsu onsen

群馬県　Gunma

❺ 伊香保温泉
ikaho onsen

群馬県　Gunma

❻ 箱根湯本温泉
hakoneyumoto onsen

神奈川県　Kanagawa

❼ 熱海温泉
atami onsen

静岡県　Shizuoka

❽ 伊東温泉
itoo onsen

静岡県　Shizuoka

❾ 下呂温泉
gero onsen

岐阜県　Gifu

❿ 白浜温泉
shirahama onsen

和歌山県　Wakayama

⓫ 別府温泉
beppu onsen

大分県　Ooita

⓬ 湯布院温泉
yuhuin onsen

大分県　Ooita

Kinds of Bath（風呂の種類）

打たせ湯
utaseyu
cascading water

蒸し風呂
mushiburo
steam bath

砂風呂
sunaburo
sand bath

PART3

24 Buying Souvenirs

おみやげを買う
omiyage wo kau

What's this?
これは何ですか？
kore wa nandesuka

kore wa nandesuka ?

Typical Souvenirs（代表的なおみやげ）

扇子
sensu
fan

うちわ
uchiwa
round fan

茶碗
chawan
teacup

お盆
obon
tray

つぼ
tsubo
pot

手ぬぐい
tenugui
towel

風呂敷
huroshiki
wrapping cloth

着物
kimono
clothing

風鈴
huurin
wind-bell

羽子板
hagoita
battledore

はし
hashi
chopsticks

こけし
kokeshi
wooden doll

浴衣
yukata
summer informal
cotton kimono

半纏
hanten
short coat

かんざし
kanzashi
ornamental
hairpin

招き猫
manekineko
cat inviting
guests & luck

"The reality always falls short of the reputation" in Japanese is "meibutsu ni

Do you have anything interesting?
めずらしい物はありませんか？
mezurashii mono wa arimasenka

What's a specialty here?
ここの名産は何ですか？
koko no meisan wa nandesuka

Two of these, please.
これを2つください。
kore wo hutatsu kudasai

けんだま
kendama
cup and ball

下駄
geta
clogs

でんでん太鼓
dendendaiko
small drum

万華鏡
mangekyoo
kaleidoscope

ちょうちん
choochin
lantern

掛け軸
kakejiku
hanging picture

のれん
noren
shop curtain

折り紙
origami
colored folding paper

Did you know? (知ってましたか?)

Furoshiki (wrapping cloth) was used for wrapping your clothes when you took a bath and after taking a bath used for drying your feet in old times.

●風呂敷は昔、お風呂に入るときに着ていた物を包み、お風呂から出たあとにそれで足を拭くのに使われていました。

いっしょだね

---

umaimono nashi". (→和訳)　　　　"名物にうまいものなし"ということわざがある。　**57**

25 Kabuki

歌舞伎
kabuki

What's Kabuki? (歌舞伎ってなに？)

It has a tradition over 400 years.
● 400年以上の伝統があります。
It is performed only by male actors.
● 男性だけで演じます。
The stage floor is equipped with a revolving stage and a trapdoor.
● 舞台には、回り舞台やせりなどの工夫がされています。

Words about Kabuki stage (舞台装置などの名称)

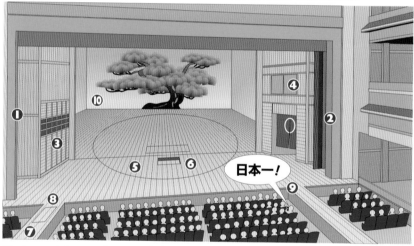

日本一！

❶ stage right
下手
shimote

❷ stage left
上手
kamite

❸ musician's box
下座
geza

❹ chorus box
ちょぼ床
choboyuka

❺ revolving stage
回り舞台
mawaributai

❻ trapdoor
せり
seri

❼ elevated runway
花道
hanamichi

❽ trapdoor
すっぽん
suppon

❾ shout
かけ声
kakegoe

❿ painted scenery and props
かきわり
kakiwari

⓫ stagehand dressed in black
黒衣
kurogo

Red kabuki make-up shows a good man, and black shows a bad man or a god. (→和訳)

male actors playing female roles
女形(女役の男優)
oyama(on-nagata)

male-role actors
立役
(男役の男優)
tachiyaku

hero
荒事師
aragotoshi

a man with super-human power.
●超人的なパワーを持つ。

handsome man
和事師
wagotoshi

appears in love plays.
●恋愛などの劇に登場。

kabuki make-up
隈取
kumadori

二本隈
nihonguma

半隈
hanguma

火炎隈
kaenguma

Did you know?(知ってましたか?)

Why is kabuki only played by male actors? It is said a lady called "Okuni" started "Okuni-kabuki" early in the 17th century. But the government forbade it, because it was a little too erotic. Since then, kabuki has been played only by men.

●なぜ、男だけでやるようになったのでしょうか？ "阿国" という女性が17世紀初めに始めた "阿国歌舞伎" が、好色的でありすぎるなどの理由で禁止され、それ以来、男子だけで演じることになったのです。

隈取のなかでも、紅隈は善人を、墨隈は悪人や神を表している。

26 Noh & Kyoogen

能と狂言
noo to kyoogen

What's Noh? (能ってなに？)

Noh is the oldest of Japan's theatrical
arts incorporating music, dances and plays.
●能は日本最古の音楽劇です。
Noh was established at the beginning of the 14th century
(Muromachi period).
●14世紀(室町時代)の初めに確立されました。
Noh was completed by Kan-ami and Zeami, a father and a son.
●観阿弥(かんあみ)、世阿弥(ぜあみ)の親子によって大成されました。

Noh-masks (能面)

female
女面
on-namen

**female
demon**
般若
han-nya

**old
man**
尉面
joo
men

Words about Noh & Kyoogen stage (舞台装置などの名称)

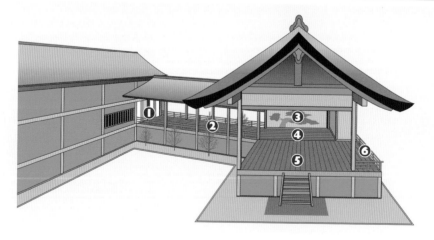

Even the Japanese sometimes don't understand the old Japanese language which is used in

What's Kyoogen? (狂言ってなに？)

Kyoogen is a traditional comedy based on daily life.
●狂言は、日常の笑いをドラマにしたものです。
Only some of the players put on a mask.
●面をつけるのは、一部の役者だけです。

"Taroo-kaja" is a servant and representative of people.
●太郎冠者(たろうかじゃ)は召使いで、庶民の代表です。
Hon-kyoogen is performed independently.
●本(ほん)狂言は、独立して演じられます。
Ai-kyoogen is performed between Noh plays.
●間(あい)狂言は、能と能の間に演じられます。

Kyoogen-masks (狂言の面)

fox
狐
kitsune

monkey
猿
saru

God of wealth
恵比寿
ebisu

❶ curtain
揚幕
agemaku

❷ bridge
橋掛かり
hashigakari

❸ scene panel
鏡板
kagamiita

❹ rear stage
後座
atoza

❺ main stage
舞台
butai

❻ chorus area
地謡座
jiutaiza

main character
シテ(主役)
shite(shuyaku)

supporting character
ワキ(脇役)
waki(wakiyaku)

神楽と文楽

kagura to bunraku

What's Kagura? (神楽ってなに?)

Kagura is music and dance dedicated to the Gods of Shinto.

●神楽は、神様(神道)に捧げる音楽と踊りです。

Mi-kagura is ancient court dance and music since 11th century.

●御神楽は、11世紀から伝わる古代の宮中の踊りと音楽です。

Sato-kagura is performed at the local shrines.

●里神楽(さとかぐら)は、その地方の神社などで演じられます。

獅子舞
shishimai
lion dance

おかめ(阿亀)
okame
Young woman.
okame mask is used
in kagura and kabuki.
●若い女性。おかめの
面は神楽や歌舞伎で
使われる。

ひょっとこ
hyottoko
Hyottoko is from the
word "hi-otoko"(fire man)
breathing fire.
●"ひょっとこ"は"火男"か
らきている。口をとがら
せて火をおこしている。

天狗
tengu
monster with
supernatural
powers.
●超自然的な
パワーを持
つ怪物。

What's Bunraku? (文楽ってなに?)

Bunraku is the traditional Japanese puppet theater.
●文楽は、日本の伝統的な人形芝居です。
A doll is manipulated by three puppeteers.
●ひとつの人形を3人であやつります。
They move the eyes, eyebrows and mouth by strings.
●目と眉と口は、糸で操作して動かします。

Bunraku stage (文楽の舞台)

主遣い
omozukai
for the head and the
rigtht hand
●顔の表情と右手を動
かす

左遣い
hidarizukai
for the left hand
●左手を動かす

足遣い
ashizukai
for the legs
●足を動かす

Female puppets have no legs.
●女の人形には足がありません。

若男
waka-otoko
young man

娘
musume
young girl

がぶ
gabu
demon

雅楽と邦楽

gagaku to hoogaku

What's Gagaku & Hoogaku?（雅楽・邦楽ってなに？）

Gagaku is court music which has performed since Heian period(794～1192).

●雅楽は平安時代からの宮廷音楽です。

They use unique musical instruments to perform Gagaku.

●雅楽は、独特の楽器を使って演奏されます。

Hoogaku is music which is performed with a banjo-like instrument and a bamboo flute.

●邦楽は三味線や尺八などによる音楽のことです。

Musical instruments（楽器）

banjo-like instrument
三味線
shamisen

bamboo flute
尺八
shakuhachi

plectrum
ばち
bachi

small drum
鼓
tsuzumi

Japanese harp
琴
koto

drum
太鼓
taiko

wind instrument
笙
shoo

Japanese mandolin
琵琶
biwa

㉙ Variety Theater

寄席

yose

What's Yose? (寄席ってなに？)

Yose is a small theater where you can enjoy rakugo, manzai and kyokugei.
●寄席は、落語や漫才、曲芸などが行われる小さな劇場です。
Each entertainment has a traditional program and a modern one.
●どの芸も伝統的な出し物と現代的な出し物があります。

落語 rakugo

Rakugo is the art of comic storytelling which has been performed since Edo Period(1603～1868). A performer in kimono tells stories with humorous gestures.
●落語は、江戸時代から演じられてきたおもしろい話芸です。着物を着た落語家が、ゆかいな身振り手振りで話をします。

漫才 manzai

Manzai is comic dialogues.
●漫才とは、おもしろおかしい会話です。

Juggling on the umbrella
傘回し
kasa mawashi

曲芸 kyokugei

Juggling, acrobatics.
●物を投げる芸や軽業のことです。

Bamboo blind tricks
玉すだれ
tama sudare

講談 koodan

Koodan is historical narrative. The storyteller performs by tapping a small table(shakudai) in front of him with a fan in hand.
●講談は歴史的な説話です。講釈師は、釈台を扇子で叩きながら演じます。

浪曲 rookyoku

Rookyoku is recitation with shamisen music.
●歴史的な物語を三味線の伴奏で語り、歌います。

雅楽で使われている音楽は、現存する合奏音楽では世界最古といわれている。

PART4

③⓪ Flower Arrangement or Ikebana

華 道
kadoo

What's Kadoo?（華道ってなに？）

A tradition since the 16th century, there are now three major "ikebana" schools, Ikenoboo, Ohara and Soogetsu.

●16世紀以来の伝統を持ち、現在、池坊（いけのぼう）、
　小原（おはら）、草月（そうげつ）の3大流派があります。

What's this style?
これはどんなスタイルですか？
kore wa don-na sutairu desuka

This is Nage-ire.
これは "投げ入れ" といいます。
kore wa "nageire" to iimasu

slanting style
投げ入れ
nageire

Does it mean anything?
何か意味があるのですか？
nanika imi ga arunodesuka

upright style
盛り花
moribana

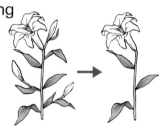

It shows the natural shape of flowers.
花の自然な姿をあらわしています。
hana no shizen na sugata wo arawashite imasu

Basic techniques（基本技術）

cut
切る
kiru

trimming
さばく
sabaku

Cut the stem under water to increase water absorption.
●水の深いところで切ると、水圧で花材が水をよく吸い上げる。

Remove unnecessary leaves and twigs to make beautiful arrangement.
●美しく生けるために、不要な葉や小枝を取り除く。

Materials (材料)

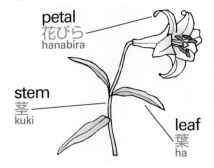

petal
花びら
hanabira

stem
茎
kuki

leaf
葉
ha

bud
つぼみ
tsubomi

twig
小枝
koeda

Utensils (道具)

basin
水盤
suiban

spiked holder
剣山
kenzan

scissors
はさみ
hasami

atomizer
霧吹き
kirihuki

vase
花器
kaki

pot
つぼ
tsubo

basket
かご
kago

saw
のこぎり
nokogiri

wire
はりがね
harigane

bending
ためる
tameru

Bend the stem to arrange easily.
●生けやすいように、茎や枝を曲げる。

fixing
留める
tomeru

Cut ends of the branch to insert them into the spiked holder easily.
●剣山にさしやすいように、切り込みを入れる。

（→和訳）日本人はさくらんぼを食べ、塩漬けの桜の花を桜湯に、桜餅には塩漬けの葉を巻いて食べる。

PART4

31 Tea Ceremony

茶 道
sadoo

What's Sadoo? (茶道ってなに？)

Tea Ceremony was perfected by Sen-no-Rikyuu in the 16th century.
●茶道は16世紀ごろ、千利休によって大成されました。
We enjoy tea following the traditional manners.
●伝統的な作法に従って、お茶を楽しみます。

❶ the water is discarded after washing the tea bowl
建水
kensui

❷ water ladle
ひしゃく
hishaku

❸ kettle
釜
kama

❹ brazier
風炉
huro

❺ jug of water
水差し
mizusashi

❻ tea bowl
茶碗
chawan

tea scoop
茶杓
chashaku

bamboo tea whisk
茶せん
chasen

container for powdered green tea
なつめ
natsume

How do I drink tea?
どうやってお茶を飲むのですか？
dooyatte ocha wo nomuno desuka

Just follow my example.
私のまねをしなさい。
watashi no mane wo shinasai

A small tea ceremony room has a small entrance which is about sixty centimeters

How to drink tea（お茶の飲み方）

❶ Lift the chawan with the right hand and place it on the left palm.
茶わんを右手で取り上げ、左の手のひらに乗せる。

❷ Rotate the chawan clockwise three times.
時計まわりに、茶わんを3回まわす。

❸ Drink the tea quietly.
静かにお茶を飲む。

❹ Wipe the chawan with the fingers.
指で茶わんをふき取る。

❺ Rotate the chawan counterclockwise three times.
逆時計まわりに、茶わんを3回まわす。

❻ Express your thanks.
感謝を表現する。

Did you know?（知ってましたか?）

At the tea party, you have to be careful not to step on the border of tatami mat and it is the manner to say "Kekkoo na otemae deshi ta. (It was a good tea.) " after tasting tea.

●お茶の席では、畳のふちを踏まないこと、お茶をいただいたあとは「結構なお点前でした」と言うのがマナーです。

PART4

32 Bonsai

盆 栽
bonsai

What's Bonsai? (盆栽ってなに？)

Bonsai is the horticultural art of miniature potted trees and plants.

●盆栽は、鉢に小さい木などを植えて楽しむものです。

Shape of Bonsai (盆栽の形)

直 幹
chokkan
upright style

斜 幹
shakan
slanting style

懸 崖
kengai
cascading style

文人木
bunjinboku
a few branches style

石付き
ishizuki
rock planting style

Occasional cutting of roots of the bonsai help it grow small. (→和訳)

How old is this tree?
この木はどのくらいたっているのですか？
kono ki wa donokurai tatteiruno desuka

It's about fifteen years old.
15年くらいたっています。
juugo-nen kurai tatte imasu

How do you take care of this "Bonsai"?
どのように世話をするのですか？
donoyooni sewa wo suruno desuka

Words about Bonsai（関連単語）

❶ pruning
剪定
sentei

❷ transplanting
植え替え
uekae

❸ wiring
針金かけ
harigane-kake

scissors	saw	funnel	wire
はさみ	のこぎり	じょうご	針金
hasami	nokogiri	joogo	harigane

Did you know?（知ってましたか?）

How to distinguish good Bonsai.
① good roots spreading in all directions. ② good balance of branches. ③ expressing nature.
●よい盆栽の見分け方。
①太い根が、四方八方に張っている。②枝のバランスがいい。③自然をうまく表現している。

ときどき根を切ると、枝も葉も大きく育たない。

書道と水墨画
shodoo to suibokuga

What's Shodoo? (書道ってなに？)

Calligraphy is one of the unique arts drawing characters using a brush which is made of wool or badger hair and bamboo.

●書道は独特な芸術のひとつで、羊毛や狸（たぬき）の毛、そして竹で作られた筆を使って字を書きます。

Tools (道具)

❶ brush
筆
hude

❷ paper weight
文鎮
bunchin

❸ plain writing paper
半紙
hanshi

❹ inkstone
硯
suzuri

❺ ink stick
墨
sumi

❻ underlay
下敷き
shitajiki

❼ water container
水差し
mizusashi

Show me an example, please.

何かひとつ書いてください。
nanika hitotsu kaite kudasai

What's Suibokuga? (水墨画ってなに？)

Suibokuga is painted in Indian ink and images are made only with shading of the ink.

●水墨画は墨で描かれ、絵は墨の濃淡だけで表現されます。

〈Toukeizu(winter scenery)・
　Sesshuu (1420〜1506.
　　　　　　　　Muromachi period)〉

Sesshuu (A famous painter and Zen priest) This is one of the most important works of Sesshuu.

●〈冬景図・雪舟
　　　（1420〜1506・室町時代）〉
　雪舟は有名な画家で、禅僧でもありました。これは彼の代表的な作品のひとつです。

Did you know? (知ってましたか？)

It is said that a master calligrapher knows everything about someone's character and mind by seeing his work.

●書道の達人は、その人の書いた字を
　見ると、その人の性格や心の状態が
　わかるといわれています。

書道を練習することで集中力が増す。

俳 句
haiku

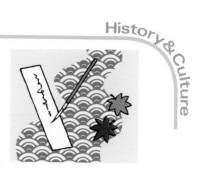

What's a Haiku? (俳句ってなに?)

Haiku is a Japanese poetic form which consists of 17 syllables (5-7-5 syllables) and has to contain "kigo"(a word that expresses a season).

●俳句は、日本の詩です。17音節(5−7−5音節)からできていて、必ず "季語" を含んでいます。

Famous Haikus? (有名な俳句)

朝顔につるべ取られてもらい水
asagao ni tsurube torarete moraimizu ※1

Taken by the morning glory, the well bucket, I have to ask someone for water.

●井戸のつるべに巻きついた朝顔があまりに可憐なので、取り払うことができずに近所に水をもらいに行く。

kigo : morning glory   season : fall (季語:朝顔   季節:秋)

やれ打つな蝿が手をする足をする ※2
yare utsuna hae ga te wo suru ashi wo suru

Don't hit, a fly is begging your pardon with its hands rubbing, also feet rubbing.

●むやみに蝿を叩くな。こんなに手足をすり合わせて、謝っているではないか。

kigo : a fly   season : summer (季語:蝿   季節:夏)

雀の子そこのけそこのけお馬が通る
suzumenoko sokonoke sokonoke ouma ga tooru
　　　　　　　　　　　　　　　　　　※3

Baby sparrows, get out of the way, a horse is coming(Watch out!).

●スズメの子や、馬が通るからそこをどいてね、あぶないよ。

kigo : baby sparrows   season : spring (季語:雀の子   季節:春)

古池やかわず飛び込む水の音 ※4
huruikeya kawazu tobikomu mizu no oto

An old pond,the sound of water, a frog jumps in.

●あたりの静寂をやぶって、古池にかわず（かえる）の飛び込んだ音が響いている。

kigo：a frog　season：spring（季語：かわず　季節：春）

How to make a Haiku（俳句の作り方）

Kigo

❶ Decide what you want to describe.
主題を決める。

❷ Choose the kigo.
季語を選ぶ。

❸ Express your feelings in three lines of a short English poem.
3行の英語の詩で気持ちを表現する。

Did you know?（知ってましたか？）

※4 Matsuo Bashoo(1644～1694) is one of the most famous haiku poets in Japan. He traveled around the country making many haikus.

●※4の句の作者である松尾芭蕉（江戸前期の人）は、日本で最も有名な俳人の一人です。日本中を旅行して、多くの俳句を作りました。

※1 Kaga no Chiyo, a poetess(1703～1775)
　　江戸中期の女流俳人、加賀千代の作品。

※2・3 Kobayashi Issa(1763～1827)
　　江戸中期の俳人、小林一茶の作品。

日本の子どもたちは、簡単に俳句を作ることができる。

(35) Proverbs

ことわざ
kotowaza

What's Kotowazas? (ことわざってなに？)

"Kotowaza" is a proverb. Here are some Kotowazas which have similar meanings to English proverbs.

● "ことわざ" とは "proverb" のことです。ここでは、英語のことわざ に似た意味を持つ日本のことわざを紹介します。

Famous Kotowazas (有名なことわざ)

こう いん
光陰矢のごとし
kooin yano gotoshi

Time flies like an arrow.
（時間は矢のように速く飛ぶ）

猿も木から落ちる
sarumo kikara ochiru

Even Homer sometimes nods.
（かの古代ギリシャの詩人ホメロスでさえ うなずくことがある）

石の上にも3年
ishino uenimo san-nen

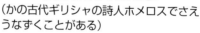

Perseverance will win in the end.
（忍耐は最後に勝つ）

Misfortunes never come singly .(proverb) （→和訳）

類は友を呼ぶ
rui wa tomo wo yobu

Birds of a feather flock together.
（同じ羽を持つ鳥は集まる）

去るものは日々に疎し
sarumono wa hibini utoshi

Out of sight, out of mind.
（目の前から消えてしまうと、思い出すことも少なくなる）

蛙の子は蛙
kaerunoko wa kaeru

Like father, like son.
（親を見ると子どもに似ているし、
子どもを見ると親に似ている）

地獄の沙汰も金しだい
jigoku no sata mo kane shidai

Money opens all doors.
（お金はすべてのドアを開けることができる）

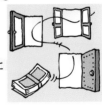

Did you know? (知ってましたか?)

There are some Japanese proverbs about the parts of the body.
●体の部分に関することわざを紹介します。

①へそで茶をわかす heso de cha wo wakasu
You can boil tea on your bellybutton. (What a joke!!)

②腹が減っては戦が出来ぬ hara ga hette wa ikusa ga dekinu
We cannot fight on an empty stomach.

③背に腹はかえられぬ se ni hara wa kaerarenu
We can't exchange our back for our belly. Necessity knows no law.

36 Nursery Tales

おとぎ話

otogibanashi

What's Otogibanashi? (おとぎ話ってなに？)

Otogibanashi is a story for children which is based on the legend or imaginary stories.
●おとぎ話は、伝説や空想をもとにした子ども向けの話です。

Otogibanashi is also called "Mukashi banashi".
●おとぎ話は“むかし話”ともいいます。

Famous Otogibanashis (有名なおとぎ話)

金太郎 kintaroo

❶ Kintaroo lived in Ashigara mountain.
足柄山の金太郎。

❷ Kintaroo with a broadax practices horse riding on a bear.
まさかりかついだ金太郎、熊にまたがりお馬の稽古(けいこ)。

❸ He also practiced sumo with wild animals.
けもの集めて相撲の稽古。

❹ He grew up to be a great samurai.
そうして大きくなって立派なサムライになりました。

Kill a spider and rain follows. (tradition) (→和訳)

桃太郎 momotaroo

❶ Momotaroo was born from a peach.
桃から生まれた桃太郎。

❷ Please give me a piece of millet dumpling.
お腰につけたキビダンゴ、ひとつ私にくださいな。

❸ I'll give it to you, if you come with me to punish the fiends.
あげましょう、あげましょう、これから鬼の征伐（せいばつ）についてくるなら。

❹ He punished the fiends and returned home with the treasure and lived happily ever after.
鬼を征伐して宝物を持ち帰り、幸せに暮らしました。

かぐや姫 kaguyahime

❶ She was born from a bamboo.
かぐや姫は竹から生まれました。

❷ She grew up to be a beautiful lady. Many young men wanted to marry her.
かぐや姫は美しく成長し、多くの若い男性は、彼女と結婚したがりました。

❸ She gave them difficult problems.
かぐや姫は男たちに結婚のための難しい課題を出しました。

❹ She returned to the moon, her home.
そして、月に帰って行きました。

年中行事
nenchuu gyooji

Jan.1~7
1/1~1/7

The New Year
お正月
oshoogatsu

We also have a family reunion at this time.
●家族の集まるときでもあります。

Feb.3
2/3

Bean-throwing Ceremony
節分
setsubun

Driving away demons and draw in happiness. Eat as many beans as your age.
●鬼を追い払い、福を招き入れるために豆をまきます。自分の歳の数だけ豆を食べます。

July.7
7/7

The Star Festival
七夕
tanabata

It's based on the legend with Altair (Aquila) and Vega (Lyra). Write down your wishes on strips of fancy paper.
●牽牛(けんぎゅう)星(鷲座)と織女(しょくじょ)星(琴座)の伝説にもとづいたお祭りです。短冊に願いごとを書いて、笹に飾ります。

July
7/13~15 or 8/13~15

Bon Festival
お盆
obon

A Buddhist event.　At this time, the spirits of ancestors are said to return home.
●仏教の行事です。この時期に、先祖の魂が家に戻ってくると言われています。

Mar.3
3/3

Girls' Festival
ひな祭
hinamatsuri

Families with girls celebrate their daughters' good health and growth.
● 女の子のいる家庭では、ひな人形を飾って健康と成長を祝います。

May.5
5/5

Children's Day
こどもの日
kodomo no hi

Families with boys display the dolls and put up carp streamers to pray for success in life.
● 男の子のいる家庭では、人形を飾り、鯉のぼりを立てて立身出世を祈ります。

Sep.
in the middle of September
9月中旬

Moon viewing
お月見
otsukimi

Enjoy viewing the full moon and celebrate the good harvest.
● 満月を愛(め)で、豊作を祝います。

Nov.
in the middle of November
11月中旬

Festival day for 3,5 and 7 year old children
七五三
shichigosan

It's for 5 year old sons and 3 and 7 year old daughters.
● 5歳の男の子、3歳と7歳の女の子のためのお祝いの行事です。

Dec.31
12/31

New Year's Eve
大晦日(おおみそか)
oomisoka

toshi-koshi-soba (buckwheat noodles) for saying good by to the old year.
● 年越しそばを食べて、古い年にさようならを言います。

and the relatives, etc. (→和訳) お正月には、子どもたちは親、親戚などから "お年玉" をもらえる。

38 Festivals & Fairs

祭りと縁日
matsuri to en-nichi

What's Matsuri? (祭りってなに？)

There are many kinds of festivals all over Japan and they mainly carry portable shrines.

●日本の各地でいろいろな祭りが行われます。御輿(みこし)をかつぐことが多いのです。

Why are they carrying a portable shrine? It's the palanquin of a god.

●どうして御輿をかつぐのでしょうか？　御輿は神様の乗り物だからです。

portable shrine
御輿
mikoshi

float
山車
dashi

Costume for festival (祭り装束)

❶ headband
はちまき
hachimaki

❷ happi coat
はっぴ
happi

❸ long johns
股引
momohiki

❹ Japanese style socks
足袋
tabi

❺ sandals
雪駄
setta

They're saying, "wasshoi!, wasshoi!" or "soiya! soiya!" when they're carrying a portable shrine.

●御輿をかつぐときは、「ワッショイ！ワッショイ！」あるいは「ソイヤ！ソイヤ！」などと言います。

Sake is said to be indispensable in Japanese festivals to make our sense of unity with

What's En-nichi? (縁日ってなに?)

En-nichi fairs are held in the grounds of the shrines or the temples with many kinds of stands. Especially in the evening, they are very crowded with people.

●縁日は神社や寺の境内(けいだい)で催され、たくさんの屋台が並び、夜には多くの人が集まります。

Stand (屋台)

scooping gold fish
金魚すくい
kingyosukui

hooking yoyos
ヨーヨー釣り
yooyootsuri

shooting booth
射的屋
shatekiya

hitotsu choodai
One, please

Why don't we drop in at that stand?
屋台に行きましょう。
yatai ni ikimashoo

One, please.
ひとつちょうだい。
hitotsu choodai

foam candy
カルメラ焼き
karumerayaki

bekko candy
べっこうあめ
bekkooame

cotton candy
わたあめ
wata-ame

rice-cracker with sauce
ソースせんべい
soosu senbei

chow mein
焼きそば
yakisoba

God deeper. (→和訳)　　　神様との一体感を深めるために、日本の祭りには酒が欠かせない。　**83**

㊴ Lacquerware & Ceramics

漆器と陶磁器

shikki to toojiki

What's Shikki? (漆器ってなに？)

Lacquerware is a container coated with lacquer.

●漆器とは、漆（うるし）を塗った器です。

Lacquer gives a container gloss and protects it from rotting and humidity.

●漆は器に光沢を与え、腐食や湿気から守る働きがあります。

Process (工程)

❶ forming wood
木地作り
kiji zukuri

❷ preparing the surface
下地作り
shitaji zukuri

❸ undercoating
下地塗り
shitaji nuri

❹ final coating
上塗り
uwanuri

❺ decoration
加飾
kashoku

inlay gold powder
沈金
chinkin

sprinkle gold or silver powder over the picture.
蒔絵
makie

using shells
螺鈿
raden

What's Toojiki? (陶磁器ってなに？)

A rice bowl is a kind of Toojiki.
- お茶わんは陶磁器の一種です。

Toojiki is also called "Setomono", it was originally from Seto-pottery.
- 陶磁器のことを"瀬戸物"とも言いますが、これは有名な"瀬戸焼"からきています。

Process (工程)

❶ shaping
形作り

katachi zukuri

❷ fired without glazing
素焼き
suyaki

❸ picture drawings
絵付け
etsuke

❹ last firing
焼き上げ
yakiage

Did you know? (知ってましたか？)

If you touch the leaves of the urushi tree, you'll get a rash.
- 漆の葉に触れると、かぶれることがあります。

Sometimes they coat a container with lacquer tens of times.
- 物によっては、器に漆を数十回、乾いたら塗るということをします。

When you handle lacquerware, be careful of the following.
- 漆器を扱うときは次のことに注意しましょう。

英語では、漆も漆器のことも"Japan"と言う。

40 Ukiyoe

浮世絵
ukiyoe

What's Ukiyoe?（浮世絵ってなに？）

Ukiyoe are wood-block prints depicting this enjoyable world.
●浮世絵は、この楽しい浮き世を描いた木版画です。
They are the prints of actors, beauties, landscapes, famous courtesans and some erotic prints called "makurae".
●役者、美人、風景、おいらん、"枕絵" と呼ばれるちょっとエロティックなものもあります。

Kinds of Ukiyoe（浮世絵の種類）

samurais, sumo-wrestlers
武者絵
musha-e

beauties
美人画
bijin-ga

喜多川歌麿
Kitagawa Utamaro

actors
役者絵
yakusha-e

東洲斎写楽
Tooshuusai Sharaku

half erotic pictures
あぶな絵
abuna-e

landscapes
風景画
huukei-ga

安藤広重
Andoo Hiroshige

erotic pictures
枕絵
makura-e

The first two hundred Ukiyoe printings are more expensive than those which were printed

How to make Ukiyoe print（浮世絵ができるまで）

 painter
絵師
eshi

 carver
彫り師
horishi

 **printer**
摺り師
surishi

❶ drawing a draft and a block copy.
絵師が下絵と版下を描く。

❷ engraving the block and printing in black.
彫り師がそれを彫り、墨1色で摺る。

cherry wood

❸ indicating the colors.
絵師が色を指定する。

❹ carving a block per color.
彫り師が1色ごとに1枚の版木に彫る。

❺ printing on the same paper color by color.
摺り師が同じ紙に、色の数だけ摺っていく。

Did you know?（知ってましたか?）

In the Edo period, Ukiyoe was used as wrapping paper for Japanese ceramics exported to Europe. European people were very surprised by Ukiyoe's beauty. Ukiyoe greatly influenced van Gogh and Claude Monet. This was how Ukiyoe became world-wide popular.

●江戸時代、浮世絵はヨーロッパに輸出された日本の陶芸品の包装紙として使われていました。ヨーロッパの人たちは浮世絵の美しさに驚いたと言います。また、ゴッホ、モネなどに大きな影響を与えました。こうして、浮世絵は世界中に広まっていきました。

afterwards. (→和訳) 浮世絵は最初の約200枚のものが大切。そのあとのものとでは、値段に差が出る。

④ Origami

折り紙

origami

What's Origami? (折り紙ってなに？)

Origami is folding up various shapes without using paste or scissors.
●折り紙は、のりもはさみも使わずにいろいろなものを折ります。

How to fold a samurai helmet (かぶとの折り方)

❶ A piece of square paper.
正方形の紙を1枚用意する。

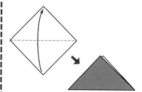

❷ Make a triangle.
三角形を作る。

❸ Back to a smaller square.
小さな正方形にもどる。

❹ Fold up to each symbol.
印に合わせて折り上げる。

❺ Fold back a little like this.
少し斜めに折り返す。

❻ Fold up the facing flap.
上の1枚を折り上げる。

❼ Fold the same flap again.
もう1回折り上げる。

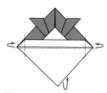

❽ Fold the other flap inside.
下の1枚を内側に折りたたむ。

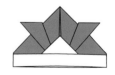

❾ A samurai helmet!!
かぶとの完成!!

Let's make sumo-wrestlers and play with them.
力士を作って遊びましょう。
rikishi wo tsukutte asobimashoo

I'll show you how to make a sumo-wrestler.
力士の作り方を教えてあげます。
rikishi no tsukurikata wo oshiete agemasu

How to fold a Sumo-Wrestler (力士の折り方)

❶ Bring the corners to the center point.
正方形の紙を中心に向かって折る。

❷ Do ❶ again to make a smaller square.
もう一度同じように中心に向かって折り、さらに小さな正方形を作る。

❸ Turn over and fold along the diagonal line.
ひっくり返して対角線に沿って折る。

❹ Fold the other one along the diagonal line too.
片方も同じように折る。

❺ Turn over and open the upper half.
ひっくり返して上半分を開く。

❻ Open the other half too.
片方も開く。

❼ Fold down the top.
点線のところを折る。

❽ Fold up the bottom.
・印を折り上げる。

❾ Fold the both sides to the center.
図のようにたたんで完成!!

力士になるには、身長173cm以上、体重75kg以上必要。

42 Kimono

着 物
kimono

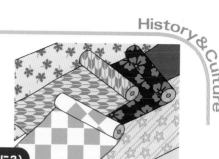

What's Kimono? (着物ってなに?)

Kimono is a beautiful and unique Japanese costume.
●着物は日本独特の美しい衣装です。
These days they are worn for ceremonial occasions such as weddings, tea ceremonies, and parties.
●最近は、おもに結婚式などの儀式やお茶会、パーティなどで着られます。

振り袖
hurisode

What a beautiful kimono!
きれいな着物ですね。
kireina kimono desune

That's furisode.
あれは、振り袖です。
are wa hurisode desu

It's a long-sleeved kimono.
袖の長い着物のことです。
sode no nagai kimono no kotodesu

For unmarried young women.
未婚の若い女性が着ます。
mikon no wakai josei ga kimasu

❶ bustle sash
帯揚げ
obiage

❷ sash cord
帯締め
obijime

❸ Japanese-style socks
足袋
tabi

❹ Japanese sandals
草履
zoori

For women (女性の着物)

留め袖
tomesode
for married women at a celebration.
●既婚女性がお祝い
の席で着るもの。

Before the "department store fire of 1932", Japanese ladies didn't wear underwear under Japanese kimono.

For men（男性の着物と帯）

with a family crest
●家紋が入っている

紋付き
montsuki
formal
●礼装

町着
machigi
less formal
●普段着

浴衣
yukata
mainly during summer.
●おもに夏の間に着るもの。

❺ **Japanese clogs**
下駄
geta

❻ **round fan**
うちわ
uchiwa

貝の口
kai no kuchi

片ばさみ
katabasami

兵児帯
heko-obi

Belt（女性の帯）

ふくら雀
hukurasuzume
〈sparrow〉

あげは蝶
agehachoo
〈butterfly〉

お太鼓
otaiko
〈drum〉

文庫
bunko
〈case〉

訪問着
hoomon-gi
for a formal visit.
●正式の訪問で着る
　もの。

浴衣
yukata
mainly during summer.
●おもに夏の間に着るもの。

without socks
素足
suashi

PART4

（→和訳）　"1932年のデパート火事"まで、日本の女性は着物の下に下着をつける習慣がなかった。

43 Zazen

座禅
zazen

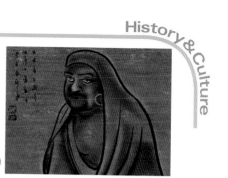

What's Zazen? (座禅ってなに?)

Zazen was originated in India and introduced to Japan by way of China in the 12th~13th century.
●座禅は、インドに発し中国を経て12〜13世紀に日本に伝わりました。
Finding the truth through concentration of the mind during Zazen.
●座ることで、精神を集中して悟りを求めます。

How to sit (正しい座り方)

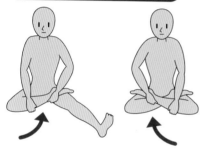

Put the right foot on the left thigh, placing the left foot on the right thigh.
●右足を左のももにのせ、左足を右のももにのせる。

半眼
han-gan
the eyes are half closed.

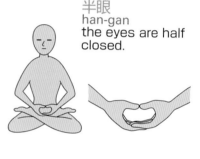

The left hand on the right hand, thumbs are touching each other.
●左の手のひらを右の手の上におき、親指をつける。

警策
kyoosaku

When the trainees lose their concentration, the trainer hits the shoulder with a kyoosaku.
●雑念が入ると、直堂(じきどう)が警策(きょうさく)で肩をたたく。

Bodhidharma was spiritually awakened after sitting against the wall for nine years. (→和訳)

(44) Ninja

忍者

ninja

What's Ninja? (忍者ってなに？)

Ninja were trained for espionage and were engaged in collecting information and assassinating (15th～16th century).

●忍者はスパイ活動のために訓練され、情報収集や暗殺などに従事しました た(15～16世紀)。

Kooga-school and Iga-school are two famous ninja schools.

●甲賀(こうが)流と伊賀(いが)流が有名です。

Weapons (武器)

手裏剣
shuriken
throwing knife

忍鎌
ninkama
sickle

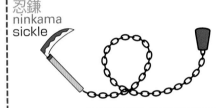

まきびし
makibishi
sharp-pointed object scattered on the road.

忍び熊手
shinobi kumade
rake

Techniques (術)

水遁の術
suiton no jutsu
hiding under water.

木遁の術
mokuton no jutsu
hinding among the trees.

45 Samurai & Castle

侍と城
samurai to shiro

What's Samurai? (侍ってなに？)

Samurai is also called "Bushi".
●侍のことを "武士" とも言います。
The Samurai government lasted for 676 years from the Kamakura government starting in 1192 to the Edo government ending in 1868.
●武士の政権は、1192年に鎌倉に幕府が開かれてから、1868年に終わった江戸幕府まで676年間続きました。

❶
❹
❷
❸

Daily Samurai (ふだんの服装)

❶ topknot
ちょんまげ
chon-mage

❷ big sword
大刀
daitoo

❸ small sword
小刀
shootoo

❹ small knife
小柄
kozuka

Samurai in the battle (戦時の服装)

❺
❻
❾
❼
❿
❽

❺ helmet
かぶと
kabuto

❻ armor
よろい
yoroi

❼ bow
弓
yumi

❽ arrow
矢
ya

❾ short coat for battle
陣羽織
jinbaori

❿ horse
馬
uma

It is said that samurais shaved the top of their heads in order to wear helmets. (→和訳)

Japanese Sword (日本刀)

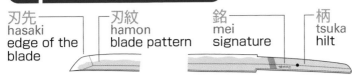

刃先
hasaki
edge of the
blade

刃紋
hamon
blade pattern

銘
mei
signature

柄
tsuka
hilt

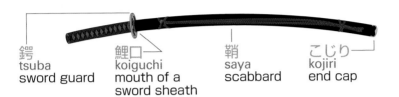

鍔
tsuba
sword guard

鯉口
koiguchi
mouth of a
sword sheath

鞘
saya
scabbard

こじり
kojiri
end cap

Japanese Castle (日本の城)

天守閣
tenshukaku
donjon

本丸
honmaru
keep of a castle

銃眼
juugan
gunports

石垣
ishigaki
stone wall

鯱(しゃちほこ)
shachihoko
dolphinlike fish,
talisman for fire

門
mon
gate

堀
hori
moat

Did you know? (知ってましたか?)

"Gen-puku" is a ceremony to celebrate one's coming of age. The children of samurai had the ceremony at the age of sixteen and they had to go to the battlefield to fight.

●"元服（げんぷく）"は一人前に成人したことを祝う儀式です。侍の子は16歳で成人と認められ、戦場に行かなくてはなりませんでした。

侍は、兜をかぶるために頭のてっぺんを剃った。

46 Sumo

相 撲
sumoo

What's Sumo? （相撲ってなに？）

To win a match, the wrestler must push his opponent out of the ring or make him fall down to the ground.

●試合に勝つためには、相手を土俵の外に押し出すか、土俵内で倒さなければなりません。

The ceremony of entering the ring （土俵入り）

行司
gyooji
referee

横綱
yokozuna
grand champion

太刀持ち
tachimochi
sword bearer

露払い
tsuyu harai
herald

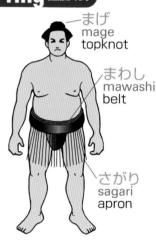

まげ
mage
topknot

まわし
mawashi
belt

さがり
sagari
apron

Techniques & Ranking （技と番付）

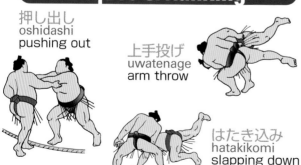

押し出し
oshidashi
pushing out

上手投げ
uwatenage
arm throw

はたき込み
hatakikomi
slapping down

Ranking

 横綱
yokozuna

 大関
oozeki

 関脇
sekiwake

 小結
komusubi

 前頭
maegashira

 十両
juuryoo

A sumo ring is a circle which is 4 meters 54 centimeters （fifteen feet） in

47 Judo

柔 道
juudoo

What's Judo? (柔道ってなに？)

Martial Arts called Juujutsu or Yawara had been transmitted since the Age of Civil Wars (15～16th). Jigoro Kano established Koodookan Judo laying the foundation on those martial arts in the early Meiji (1868～1912).

●戦国時代（15～16世紀）から伝わる柔術、柔（やわら）と呼ばれた格闘技を明治時代の初めに、嘉納治五郎が講道館柔道として大成しました。

PART4

Techniques & Uniform (技と服装)

throwing techniques
投げ技
nagewaza

巴投げ
tomoenage
round throw

一本背負い
ippon-zeoi
shoulder throw

groundwork techniques
寝技
newaza

袈裟固め
kesagatame
sash hold

joints attack techniques
関節技
kansetsu-waza

腕ひしぎ十字固め
udehishigi-juujigatame
arm bar

❶ えり
eri
collar

❷ そで
sode
sleeve

❸ 帯
obi
belt

❹ すそ
suso
bottom

空手
karate

What's Karate? (空手ってなに？)

It is thought that Chinese Kung-fu influenced the Okinawan native martial arts, and developed into present day "Karate".
●沖縄の武術が、中国の拳法の影響を受けて現在の空手として発展してきたと考えられています。
They compete by "Sparring" and "Form" during a tournament.
●空手の試合には"組み手"と"型"の2種類があります。

Techniques (技)

基本の立ち方
basic stance

受け技
block

上段受け
joodan-uke
upper level block

中段受け
chuudan-uke
middle level block

下段受け
gedan-uke
down block

手による攻撃
attackes by hands

手刀
shutoo
knife hand

貫き手
nukite
spear hand

追い突き
oizuki
step in punch

逆突き
gyakuzuki
reverse punch

蹴り技
kicks

前蹴り
maegeri
front kick

横蹴り
yokogeri
side kick

回し蹴り
mawashigeri
roundhouse kick

飛び蹴り
tobigeri
jump kick

A kiai (a shout) in Japanese martial arts gives you more power. (→和訳)

49 Aikido

合気道

aikidoo

What's Aikido? (合気道ってなに?)

Aikido was established by Morihei Ueshiba (1883～1969) who learned jujutsu.
- 合気道は、柔術を学んだ植芝盛平（うえしばもりへい　1883～1969）によって創設されました。

Aikido is better known as the art of self-defense than as of attack.
- 攻撃よりも身を守る技を重視した格闘技です。

PART4

Techniques (技)

入り身
irimi
entering

さばき
sabaki
motion

投げ技
nagewaza
throwing tech-
niques

固め技
katamewaza
controlling
techniques

Did you know? (知ってましたか?)

Samurai said "Don't draw your sword without good reason".
- 侍（さむらい）は「刀はみだりに抜くものではない」と言いました。

"There's no first strike in Karate" is the famous maxim which was taught by the karate master Gichin Funakoshi.
- 船越義珍（ふなこしぎちん）翁の有名な格言に「空手に先手なし」（相手を害する心を持ってはいけない）があります。

剣 道
kendoo

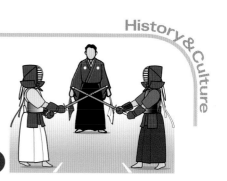

What's Kendo? (剣道ってなに?)

Kendo came from Kenjutsu(swordsmanship) which was only for samurai.

●剣道は、侍(さむらい)だけのものであった剣術がもとになっています。

Samurai used a real sword but now a bamboo sword is used in a match.

●侍は本当の刀を使いましたが、今は
竹刀(しない)が試合で使われています。

Techniques (技)

Protectors (防具)

面打ち
men-uchi
hitting
head

胴打ち
doo-uchi
hitting
torso

小手打ち
kote-uchi
hitting
forearm

突き
tsuki
thrusting
throat

❶ mask
面
men

❷ throat protector
突き垂れ
tsukidare

❸ neck and shoulder protector
面垂れ
mendare

❹ chest protector
胴
doo

❺ arm guard
小手
kote

❻ waist protector
垂れ
tare

❼ skirt-like trousers
袴
hakama

❽ bamboo sword
竹刀
shinai

51 Kyuudoo

弓 道

kyuudoo

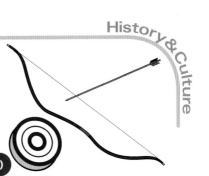

What's Kyuudoo? (弓道ってなに？)

Japanese archery originated in ancient times and some schools were established in the Middle Ages(12～17th century).

●日本の弓道は古代から行われ、中世(12～17世紀)にはいろいろな流派が生まれました。

How to shoot (矢を射る)

弦
tsuru
bowstring

矢
ya
arrow

弓懸
yugake
deerskin
glove

やじり
yajiri
arrowhead

羽
hane
feather

弓
yumi
bow

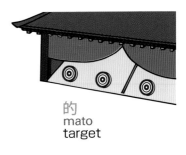

的
mato
target

Did you know? (知ってましたか？)

In 1185, in the war of Yashima, Nasuno-Yoichi succeeded in shooting the target of the fan on the boat.

●1185年に、那須与一（なすのよいち）は屋島の戦いで船の上の的を射た。

During sporting events in Japan, we are divided into two color groups : red and white. It stems from a 900 hundred year old tradition since two samurai families, Genji (family color white) and Heike (red) had a war.

●運動会の紅白は、900年くらい前、源氏は白、平家は赤で戦った名残です。

PART4

日本の伝統料理①

nihon no dentoo ryoori

Typical Japanese Food（代表的な日本料理）

すきやき
sukiyaki
hotpot of meat and vegetables

てんぷら
tempura
deep-fried fish and vegetables

寿司
sushi
fish on vinegared rice

刺し身
sashimi
raw fish

とんかつ
tonkatsu
pork cutlet

懐石料理
kaiseki ryoori
traditional dinner for a tea ceremony

What's this?
これはなんですか？
kore wa nandesuka

This one, please.
これをください。
kore wo kudasai

What's your suggestion?
何がいいか教えてください。
nani ga iika oshiete kudasai

Hotpot (なべ料理)

なべ奉行
nabe bugyoo

しゃぶしゃぶ
shabushabu
thin slices of beef and vegetables

a person who wants to take care of the pot dish

寄せ鍋
yosenabe
seafood,chicken, vegetables hotpot

水炊き
mizutaki
pot dish (chicken, vegetables, tofu)

石狩鍋
ishikarinabe
salmon, salmon roe, vegetables hotpot

Other Japanese food (そのほかの日本料理)

おでん
oden
Japanese hotch-potch

蒲焼き
kabayaki
broiled eel

串揚げ
kushiage
deep-fried food on bamboo skewers

焼き鳥
yakitori
grilled chicken on a stick

鉄板焼き
teppan-yaki
grilled on hot plate (meat,fish,vegetables)

PART5

日本の伝統料理②

nihon no dentoo ryoori

Rice bowls（どんぶりもの）

A bowl of rice with some toppings.
●ごはんの上に具がのっています。

親子丼
oyakodon
eggs and chicken rice bowl

カツ丼
katsudon
pork cutlet rice bowl

天丼
tendon
tempura rice bowl

うな丼
unadon
broiled eels rice bowl

牛丼
gyuudon
beef rice bowl

鉄火丼
tekkadon
raw tuna rice bowl

We're still waiting for our food.
（料理は）まだですか？
(ryoori wa)mada desuka

I didn't order this.
これは注文していません。
kore wa chuumon shiteimasen

Check , please.
お勘定をお願いします。
okanjoo wo onegai shimasu

It was great!
とてもおいしかったです！
totemo oishikatta desu

Noodles（うどんとそば）

うどん
udon
noodles

そば
soba
buck wheat
noodles

★ means both "udon" and "soba".
●★は "うどん" と "そば" の両方があります。

★ かけ
kake
only(buckwheat)noodles served hot

★ ざる
zaru
buckwheat noodles on a bamboo tray

★ きつね
kitsune
topped with pieces of fried bean curd

★ たぬき
tanuki
topped with fried tempura batter crusts

★ てんぷら
tempura
topped with tempura

★ 月見
tsukimi
with a raw egg

★ 鴨南蛮
kamo nanban
duck meat noodles in soy-flavored broth

カレーうどん
karee udon
noodles in curry

鍋焼きうどん
nabeyaki udon
hot noodles pot

You can make a noise when you eat udon and soba.
●うどん・そばを食べるときは、音を立ててもかまいません。

OK!
ZURU
ZURU

PART5

Sushi

sushi

What's good today?
今日は何がおいしいですか？
kyoo wa naniga oishii desuka

Toro (fatty tuna), please.
トロを握ってください
toro wo nigitte kudasai

How to eat Sushi（寿司の食べ方）

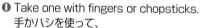

❶ Take one with fingers or chopsticks.
手かハシを使って、

❷ Dip the topping in soy sauce.
しょうゆはネタにつける。

How to make Sushi（寿司の作り方）

❶ Add vinegar to the rice while it is hot.
ごはんが熱いうちに酢を入れて混ぜる。

❷ Cool the rice off by mixing.
混ぜながらごはんを冷ます。

❸ Squeeze one bite-size sushi-meshi.
ひと口サイズに寿司めしを取る。

❹ Press the topping onto the rice.
ネタといっしょに握りこむ。

Some expensive sushi bars are said to decide the bill according to the customer's appearance.

Jargon at the Sushi bar（寿司屋の隠語）

soy sauce
しょうゆ→むらさき
shooyu　　　murasaki

ginger
しょうが→がり
shooga　　gari

green tea
お茶→あがり
ocha　　agari

Kinds of Sushis（寿司の種類）

fatty tuna
とろ
toro

gizzard shad
こはだ
kohada

prawn
えび
ebi

octopus
たこ
tako

salmon roe
いくら
ikura

sea urchin
うに
uni

conger eel
あなご
anago

squid
いか
ika

ark shell
あかがい
akagai

sea bream
たい
tai

tuna
まぐろ
maguro

young yellowtail
はまち
hamachi

seaweed roll with tuna
鉄火巻き
tekkamaki

seaweed roll
のり巻き
norimaki

egg
たまご
tamago

日本の家庭料理
nihon no katei ryoori

Taste of Home Cooking（おふくろの味）

きんぴら
kimpira

burdock and carrot cooked in soy sauce, oil, sugar

肉じゃが
nikujaga

beef, potato, onion cooked in soy sauce, sake, sugar

ひじきの煮物
hijiki no nimono

simmered dish of brown algae

煮物
nimono

simmered dish

豚汁
tonjiru

pork miso soup

漬け物
tsukemono

pickles

Miso Soup（みそ汁）

bean curd
豆腐
toofu

seaweed
わかめ
wakame

potato
じゃがいも
jagaimo

shellfish
貝
kai

This is my first time.
これは初めてです。
kore wa hajimete desu

It's tasty.
おいしいです。
oishii desu

If you leave rice in your bowl, you'll lose your eyesight.(tradition) (→和訳)

Rice & Toppings in green tea（お茶漬け）

鮭茶漬け
sakechazuke
chazuke with salted salmon

たらこ茶漬け
tarakochazuke
chazuke with salted cod roe

のり茶漬け
norichazuke
chazuke with dried seaweed

On Rice（ごはんにかけて食べるもの）

pickled ume
梅干し
umeboshi

seasoned powder
ふりかけ
hurikake

fermented soybeans
納豆
nattoo

Other Home Cooking（そのほかの家庭料理）

茶碗蒸し
chawanmushi
steamed egg custard soup

焼き魚
yakizakana
grilled fish

野菜炒め
yasaiitame
stir-fried vegetables

鶏の唐揚げ
tori no karaage
deep-fried chicken

カレー
karee
curry & rice

コロッケ
korokke
croquette

I'm afraid I don't like it.
あまり好きではありません。
amari sukidewa arimasen

Have some more?
もっといかがですか？
motto ikaga desuka

はしの使い方

hashi no tsukaikata

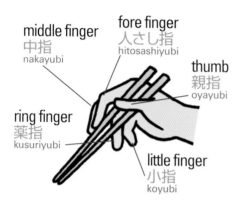

middle finger
中指
nakayubi

fore finger
人さし指
hitosashiyubi

thumb
親指
oyayubi

ring finger
薬指
kusuriyubi

little finger
小指
koyubi

Pinch the food between the upper and lower tips.
●上下のはしの間で食べ物を
　はさみます。

Bad manners (してはいけないこと)

寄せばし
yosebashi

Don't pull the dishes with chopsticks.

舐めばし
namebashi

Don't lick the tips of the chopsticks.

刺しばし
sashibashi

Don't spear food with chopsticks.

はし移し
hashiutsushi

Don't take food from another person's ch-opsticks.

迷いばし
mayoibashi

Don't dither to decide what to take next.

さぐりばし
saguribashi

Don't examine the food in the dish.

It is said that a pickled ume prevents a hangover. (→和訳)

57 How to make Onigiri(rice balls)

おにぎりの作り方

onigiri no tsukurikata

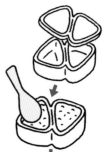

❶ Put a little salt on the palms.
手に軽く塩をつける。

❷ Put the filling on the rice.
ごはんの上に具を置く。

❸ Squeeze gently with both hands.
やさしくにぎる。

❹ Wrap with dried seaweed.
のりを巻く。

We have a rice ball maker like this.
●上のように簡単に
おにぎりを作れる
道具もある。

What's the filling of the rice ball?

おにぎりの中身は何ですか？

onigiri no nakami wa nandesuka

pickled ume
梅干し
umeboshi

salted cod roe
たらこ
tarako

salted salmon
塩鮭
shiojake

dried bonito shavings
かつおぶし
katsuobushi

梅干しには、二日酔いを防ぐ効果があるといわれている。 **111**

Food & Cooking

うどん・そば・てんぷら

udon soba tempura

How to make Udon（うどんの作り方）

❷ Make it thinner and cut in strips and then boil it.
薄くのばして細長く切り、ゆでる。

❶ Add salt and water to wheat flour and knead it.
小麦粉に塩水を加えて練る。

How to make Soba（そばの作り方）

❶ Add taro roots, egg whites to buckwheat flour.
そば粉に山芋と卵白などを加える。

❷ Make it thinner and cut in strips and then boil it.
薄くのばして細長く切り、ゆでる。

The Reserch on "Susuri-komi (sucking on)"

ズ～

ZURU ZURU

reasonable

You can make a noise when you suck in your hot noodles.
●熱い麺類を食べるときは、音を立てても かまいません。

Making a noise when you have hot noodles is not considered rude but reasonable.
●熱い麺類を食べるときに音を立てるのは、 不作法ではなく合理的です。

How to cook Tempura（てんぷらの作り方）

Dip vegetables and seafood in batter and deep-fry.
てんぷらは、野菜や魚介類に衣をつけて、高温の油で揚げたものです。

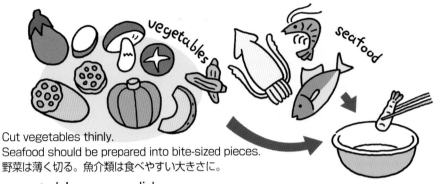

Cut vegetables thinly.
Seafood should be prepared into bite-sized pieces.
野菜は薄く切る。魚介類は食べやすい大きさに。

grated Japanese radish
大根おろし
daikon-oroshi

Deep-fry in 180℃(356F).
180℃の油で揚げる。

grated ginger
おろししょうが
oroshishooga

You have to eat Tempura right after being served.
てんぷらは揚げたてをすぐに食べること。

（すすり込みの研究）

Making a noise makes the temperature lower.
●音を立てることで、温度が下がります。

It saves you from burning your lips and tongue.
●そして、やけどをせずに熱い物をすすり込むことができるのです。

(^ ^)

air

Hot and tasty

てんぷらの語源は、ポルトガル語の "temporas（年と季節）" からきている。

59 Japanese love Soybeans

日本人は大豆が好き

nihon-jin wa daizu ga suki

Products from Soybeans (大豆から作られる物)

Bean Curd
豆腐
toohu

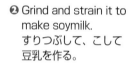

❶ Soak soybeans in water and make it soft.
大豆を水に浸してやわらかくする。

❷ Grind and strain it to make soymilk.
すりつぶして、こして豆乳を作る。

fried thin slice of tofu
油揚げ
abura-age

❸ Add some coagulating agents to make tofu.
豆乳に凝固剤を入れると豆腐ができる。

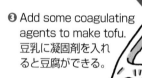

fried tofu
あつあげ
atsuage

Fermented Soybeans
納豆
nattoo
Ferment boiled soybeans with nattoo fungus.
よく煮た大豆に納豆菌を繁殖させて作る。

Can you eat natto? No

★Nattoo is said to be the hardest food to eat for foreigners.
納豆は、外国人が食べるのがいちばん難しい食べ物であると言われています。

Soy Sauce
しょうゆ
shooyu

❶ Add malted rice and salted water to soybeans and
wheat.
麹（こうじ）と食塩水を大豆
と小麦に加える。

❷ After making "moromi",it
is fermented for one year.
できたもろみを1年間発酵さ
せる。

★We also call soy sauce
"shitaji" or "murasaki".
しょうゆは "したじ" "むら
さき" とも呼ばれます。

❸ Soy sauce is extracted by
squeezing the "moromi".
それを絞るとしょうゆになる。

Soybeans Paste
味噌
miso

❶ Add malted rice and salt
to steamed soybeans.
蒸した大豆に麹と
食塩をまぜる。

❷ Ripen to make miso.
それを熟成させると味
噌ができる。

Other Soybean Products（そのほかの大豆製品）

 soybean flour
きなこ
kinako

 bean-curd refuse
おから
oakara

 top layer of boiling soymilk
湯葉
yuba

 soymilk
豆乳
toonyuu

日本人は、生タマゴにしょうゆをかけてかきまわし、熱いご飯にかけて食べるのが好き。 **115**

料理の伝統技術

ryoori no dentoo gijutsu

Cutting Techniques（いろいろな切り方）

thin slices cut
薄切り
usugiri

long thin strips cut
せん切り
sengiri

rectangles cut
短冊切り
tanzakugiri

dice cut
さいの目切り
sainomegiri

mince cut
みじん切り
mijingiri

fan cut
末広切り
suehirogiri

decorative cut
飾り切り
kazarigiri

Cut cabbage into long thin strips.
キャベツをせん切りにしてください。
kyabetsu wo sengiri ni sitekudasai

Knives（包丁のいろいろ）

vegetable knife
菜切り包丁
nakiriboochoo

kitchen knife
出刃包丁
debaboochoo

fish slicer
柳包丁
yanagiboochoo

universal knife
万能包丁
ban-nooboochoo

cutting board
まな板
manaita

This knife is very sharp.
この包丁はよく切れます。
kono hoochoo wa yoku kiremasu

調味料と香辛料

choomiryoo to kooshinryoo

 sweet
甘い
amai

 hot
辛い
karai

 sour
すっぱい
suppai

 **soy sauce**
しょうゆ
shooyu

 sugar
砂糖
satoo

 salt
塩
shio

 **ginger**
しょうが
shooga

 pepper
こしょう
koshoo

 garlic
にんにく
nin-niku

 red pepper
唐辛子
toogarashi

 vinegar
酢
su

Japanese horseradish
わさび
wasabi

PART5

A little salt, please.
塩を少し入れてください。
shio wo sukoshi iretekudasai

That's enough.
それで十分です。
sorede juubun desu

日本の ファーストフード

nihon no faasuto huudo

Let's have some fast food today.
今日はファーストフードにしましょう。
kyoo wa faasuto huudo ni shimashoo

What would you like to have?
何を食べますか？
nani wo tabemasuka

I'd like a box lunch.
弁当にします。
bentoo ni shimasu

Hamburger (ハンバーガーなど)

hamburger
ハンバーガー
hanbaagaa

pizza
ピザ
piza

sandwich
サンドイッチ
sandoicchi

fried chicken
フライドチキン
huraidochikin

french fries
フライドポテト
huraidopoteto

Chinese noodles (ラーメン)

A long line in front of the popular Chinese noodle shop.
●人気のある店には、いつも行列ができています。

味噌ラーメン
miso raamen
seasoned with soy-bean paste

しょうゆラーメン
shooyu raamen
seasoned with soy sause

塩ラーメン
shio raamen
seasoned with salt

Box Lunch (弁当)

幕の内弁当
makunouchi bentoo
with a variety of foods

ハンバーグ弁当
hanbaagu bentoo
with hamburger

とんかつ弁当
tonkatsu bentoo
with pork cutlet

しょうが焼き弁当
shoogayaki bentoo
pork sauteed with ginger

鳥唐揚げ弁当
torikaraage bentoo
with fried chicken

Eki-ben (駅弁)

Eki-ben is sold at a railroad station.
- 駅弁は、駅で売られている弁当です。

峠の釜めし
tooge no kamameshi
rice with chicken & vegetables

イカめし弁当
ikameshi bentoo
squid stuffed with rice

Others (そのほか)

お好み焼き
okonomiyaki
pancake with many kinds of ingredients

もんじゃ
monja
monja crepe

たこ焼き
takoyaki
pancake made from flour with octopus, green onion and vinegared ginger

クレープ
kureepu
crepe

(→和訳) 　日本のファーストフード店の店員は、マニュアルどおりにものを言うことが多い。　**119**

日本人の好きな食べ物

nihon-jin no sukina tabemono

Chinese & Korean food (中華・韓国料理)

餃子
gyooza
dumpling with minced pork and vegetables

しゅうまい
shuumai
steamed meat or shrimp dumpling

チャーハン
chaahan
fried rice

麻婆豆腐
maaboo doohu
tofu sauteed with ground meat

春巻き
harumaki
egg roll

焼き肉
yakiniku
Korean-style grilled meat

ビビンバ
bibinba
rice with vegetables and other ingredients

キムチ
kimuchi
Korean pickles

If you lie down right after the meals, you'll be a cow. (tradition) (→和訳)

Western food (洋食)

ハンバーグ
hanbaagu
hamburger

ステーキ
suteeki
steak

カレー
karee
curry & rice

エビフライ
ebihurai
deep-fried prawn

シチュー
shichuu
stew

スパゲティー
supagetti
spaghetti

サンドイッチ
sandoicchi
sandwiches

グラタン
guratan
gratin

チキンライス
chikinraisu
fried rice with chicken

サラダ
sarada
salad

ポタージュ
potaaju
potage

ピ　ザ
piza
pizza

食べたあとすぐに横になると、牛になる。(言い伝え)

日本酒・アルコール

nihon-shu, arukooru

Nihon-shu (日本酒)

清酒
seishu

sake

樽酒
taru
zake

barreled sake

枡酒
masu
zake

sake in
a small wooden box

こもかぶり
komokaburi

sake in a barrel wrapped
in a rush mat

sweet sake
甘口
amakuchi

hot sake
辛口
karakuchi

small sake cup
猪口
choko

sake bottle
徳利
tokkuri

How to drink Nihon-shu (日本酒の飲み方)

We have sake cold.
冷やで飲む。
hiya de nomu

We have sake hot (50〜60℃).
熱燗で飲む。
atsukan de nomu

We have sake warm (40℃).
ぬる燗で飲む。
nurukan de nomu

How to make Nihon-shu (日本酒ができるまで)

❶ Polish rice and steam it.
米を精米して蒸す。

❷ Add malted rice and water and mix them well.
麹菌（こうじきん）と水を加え、よく混ぜる。

❸ Ferment about 20days and strain the mixture.
20日ほど発酵させ、もろみをこす。

The Japanese pour beer into his friend's glass when he finds it almost empty.（→和訳）

Others（そのほかの酒）

焼酎
shoo chuu

お湯割り
oyuwari
shoochuu mixed with hot water

チューハイ
chuuhai
shoochuu and soda and fruits flavored syrup

distilled liquor made from sweet potato, rice, corn, etc.
●焼酎は、サツマイモ、米、トウモロコシなどを蒸留したものです。

梅酒
umeshu

ume liquor

ビール
biiru

beer

生ビール
nama biiru

draft beer

赤ワイン
akawain

red wine

白ワイン
shirowain

white wine

シャンペン
shanpen

champagne

ウイスキー
uisukii

whisky

水割り
mizuwari
whisky and water

オンザロック
onzarokku
whisky on the rocks

Shall we go for a drink?
飲みに行きませんか？
nomi ni ikimasenka

Do you like sake?
お酒は好きですか？
osake wa suki desuka

How about another drink?
もう1杯いかがですか？
moo ippai ikaga desuka

I can't drink anymore.
もう飲めません。
moo nomemasen

（酒の席では）相手のコップが空だったら、ビールなどをついであげる。

日本の お菓子

nihon no okashi

Sweets (甘菓子)

まんじゅう
manjuu
sweet bean-jam bun

最 中
monaka
sweet bean-jam in wafers

カステラ
kasutera
sponge cake

ようかん
yookan
a bar of sweet bean paste

おはぎ
ohagi
rice ball in sweet bean paste

かりんとう
karintoo
fried dough cookies

くずもち
kuzumochi
made from arrowroot served with sugar syrup

大判焼き
ooban-yaki
pancake stuffed with bean paste

どら焼き
dorayaki
pancake containing bean-jam

Others（そのほかの菓子類）

ところてん
tokoroten
made from agar-agar

あられ
arare
rice biscuits

せんべい
senbei
rice cracker

えびせんべい
ebisenbei
rice cracker containing shrimp

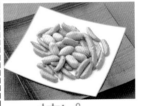

柿ピー
kakipii
tiny rice crackers and peanuts

Let's have a snack.
おやつを食べましょう。
oyatsu wo tabemashoo

Why don't you have one?
おひとついかがですか？
ohitotsu ikaga desuka

おしるこ
oshiruko
sweet red-bean soup with rice cake

だんご
dango
rice-flour dumplings put on bamboo skewers

あんみつ
anmitsu
agar-agar cubes with sweet bean paste, fruits, syrup

和菓子と呼ばれるものは、お茶といっしょに食べる。

PART5

果物と野菜
kudamono to yasai

What do you call this in Japanese (English)?
これは日本語（英語）で何と言いますか？
kore wa nihon-go (eigo) de nanto iimasuka

Fruits（果物）

peach
桃
momo

strawberry
イチゴ
ichigo

grape
ぶどう
budoo

apple
りんご
ringo

mandarin orange
みかん
mikan

water melon
スイカ
suika

melon
メロン
meron

pear
梨
nashi

persimmon
柿
kaki

cherry
さくらんぼ
sakuranbo

loquat
びわ
biwa

This persimmon is ripe enough.
この柿は、ちょうどよく熟しています。
kono kaki wa choodoyoku jukushite imasu

This avocado isn't ripe yet.
このアボカドは、まだ熟していません。
kono abokado wa mada jukushite imasen

This orange is very juicy.
このオレンジは、水分が多くておいしい。
kono orenji wa suibun ga ookute oishii

"Tochiotome" is a strawberry which is very sweet and as large as a chicken's egg. (→和訳)

Vegetables (野菜)

tomato
トマト
tomato

cucumber
きゅうり
kyuuri

green pepper
ピーマン
piiman

spinach
ほうれんそう
hoorensoo

cabbage
キャベツ
kyabetsu

bean sprouts
もやし
moyashi

green onion
ねぎ
negi

burdock
ごぼう
goboo

onion
たまねぎ
tamanegi

carrot
にんじん
ninjin

radish
大根
daikon

potato
じゃがいも
jagaimo

pumpkin
かぼちゃ
kabocha

mushroom
きのこ
kinoko

eggplant
なす
nasu

turnip
かぶ
kabu

sweet potato
さつまいも
satsumaimo

ginger
しょうが
shooga

broad bean
そら豆
soramame

bamboo shoot
竹の子
takenoko

pea
えんどう豆
endoomame

Do you have this raw?
これは生で食べるのですか？
kore wa nama de taberuno desuka

arrowhead bulb
くわい
kuwai

We have this boiled.
これは煮て食べます。
kore wa nite tabemasu

ginkgo nut
ぎんなん
gin-nan

Food & Cooking

魚と肉
sakana to niku

Fish (魚介類)

How do you cook this fish?
この魚はどうやって食べるのですか？
kono sakana wa dooyatte taberuno desuka

We bake this fish.
この魚は焼いて食べます。
kono sakana wa yaite tabemasu

We eat fish raw very often.
魚はよく生で食べます。
sakana wa yoku nama de tabemasu

sea bream
たい
tai
生 焼 煮

sardine
いわし
iwashi
生 焼 煮

flounder
かれい
karei
生 焼 煮

herring
にしん
nishin
焼 煮

trout
ます
masu
焼 煮

saury
さんま
sanma
生 焼 煮

bonito
かつお
katsuo
あ 煮

mackerel
さば
saba
し 焼 煮

yellowtail
ぶり
buri
生 焼 煮

sea bass
すずき
suzuki
生 焼 煮

生 raw　焼 baked　煮 simmered　ゆ boiled
ゆでる　あ broiled あぶる　し vinegared しめる

The eye ball of the fish contains DHA which activates our brain cells. (→和訳)

tuna
まぐろ
maguro
生 焼 煮

prawn
えび
ebi
生 ゆ

crab
かに
kani
生 ゆ

squid
いか
ika
生 ゆ 煮

octopus
たこ
tako
生 ゆ

scallop
ほたて
hotate
生 焼

Promoting Fish（出世魚）

fish that are called by different names as they grow larger.
●魚のなかには、成長とともに名前が変わるものがあります。

The story of "Buri(yellowtail)"

わかし → いなだ → わらさ → ぶり
wakashi   inada   warasa   buri

Meat（肉）

How would you like your meat?
肉はどのように焼きますか？
niku wa donoyooni yakimasuka

I'd like my steak well-done.
ステーキはよく焼いてください。
suteeki wa yoku yaite kudasai

beef
牛肉
gyuuniku

veal
子牛の肉
koushi no niku

mutton
マトン
maton

lamb
ラム
ramu

pork
豚肉
butaniku

chicken
鶏肉
toriniku

wing
手羽肉
tebaniku

gizzard
砂肝
sunagimo

duck
鴨肉
kamoniku

ground meat
ひき肉
hikiniku

魚の目玉には、DHA（ドコサヘキサエン酸）が含まれていて、脳細胞を活性化する。 **129**

家に招待する
ie ni shootai suru

❶ Meeting (待ち合わせ)

At 10!
10時に!
juu-ji ni

Let's meet at the ticket gate.
駅の改札で会いましょう。
eki no kaisatsu de aimasyoo

❷ Entrance (玄関で)

Please come in.
どうぞお入りください。
doozo ohairi kudasai

You live in a nice area.
いいところにお住まいですね。
ii tokoro ni osumai desune

❸ Living room (居間で)

Let me introduce my family.
家族を紹介します。
kazoku wo syookai shimasu

Nice to meet you.
はじめまして、よろしく。
hajimemashite yoroshiku

❹ Dinner (食事のとき)

Shall we start?
いただきます。
itadakimasu

The Japanese usually bring some small gift when they visit someone's home for the

⑤ Bath（お風呂で）

Wash yourself on the draining floor.
体は洗い場で洗ってください。
karada wa araiba de aratte kudasai

Not in the bathtub.
湯船の中ではありませんよ。
yubune no nakadewa arimasen-yo

⑥ Bed（寝るとき）

Good night.
おやすみなさい。
oyasuminasai

We have breakfast at eight.
朝食は8時です。
chooshoku wa hachi-ji desu

⑦ Others（そのほか）

Ouch!
あ痛!
a ita

Watch your head!
頭に気をつけて！
atama ni kiwo tsukete

⑧ Farewell（お別れ）

Good-bye.
さようなら。
sayoonara

Please come again!
また来てくださいね！
mata kite kudasai-ne

Thank you for everything.
いろいろとありがとうございました。
iroiroto arigatoo gozaimashita

PART6

日本の家

nihon no ie

❶ tatami mat 畳 tatami	❷ sliding door 襖（ふすま） husuma	❸ paper sliding door 障子 shooji	❹ closet 押入れ oshiire
❺ threshold 敷居 shikii	❻ ceiling 天井 tenjoo	❼ lintel 鴨居 kamoi	❽ alcove 床の間 tokonoma
❾ hanging picture 掛け軸 kakejiku	❿ vase 花びん kabin	⓫ veranda 縁側 engawa	⓬ cushion 座布団 zabuton

In a Japanese style house, don't step on the alcove. (→和訳)

enjoy each other's company
だんらん
danran

foot warmer
こたつ
kotatsu

Shinto altar
神棚
kamidana

Buddhist altar
仏壇
butsudan

Did you know?（知ってましたか？）

If you are over six feet tall, be careful when entering a room in a traditional Japanese house. This, because the height of the lintel of a room clears only six feet.

●日本間の入り口の鴨居の高さは約6フィート（180㎝）なので、それ以上の身長の人は注意が必要です。

床の間には上がらないこと。 **133**

PART6

電話をする
denwa wo suru

❶ He's in (相手がいる)

May I speak Mr.Tanaka?
田中さんはおいでに
なりますか？
tanaka-san wa oideni
narimasuka

This is James White.
ジェームス・ホワイト
です。
jeemusu-howaito desu

Who is speaking, please?
どちら様ですか？
dochirasama desuka

Hold on, please.
ちょっと
お待ちください。
chotto omachi kudasai

❷ He's out (相手が留守)

I'm sorry he is out now.
すみませんが、
彼は外出中です。
sumimasen ga
kare wa gaishutsuchuu desu

He will be back by 5.
5時ごろには
もどります。
go-ji goro niwa modorimasu

When will he be back?
何時ごろ
おもどりですか？
nanji goro
omodori desuka

❸ Message (メッセージを頼む)

May I leave a message?
伝言をお願いできますか？
dengon wo onegai dekimasuka

I'll call him again.
またあとで電話します。
mata atode denwa shimasu

I'd like him to call me.
私に電話をお願いします。
watashi ni denwa wo onegai shimasu

④ Your party is on the line （直接相手が出たら）

Is this Reina?
レイナさんですか?
reina-san desuka

This is she.
はい、そうです。
hai soodesu

This is Jack.
ジャックです。
jakku desu

⑤ Hanging up （電話を切る）

I guess I should hang up now.
そろそろ電話を
切らないと。
sorosoro denwa wo kiranaito

Thank you for your calling.
お電話ありがとう。
odenwa arigatoo

Nice talking with you.
いいえ。
iie

⑥ Wrong number （間違い電話）

What number did you call?
何番におかけですか?
nanban ni okake desuka

You have the wrong number.
間違い電話です。
machigai denwa desu

I'm sorry, I've got the wrong number.
ごめんなさい、
間違えました。
gomen-nasai
machigae mashita

⑦ Cellular phone （携帯電話）

This is my cellular phone number.
これが私の携帯の番号です。
kore ga watashi no keitai no bangoo desu

Please call my cellular phone.
私の携帯に電話してください。
watashi no keitai ni denwashite kudasai

PART6

電車などの公共の乗り物の中では、携帯電話で話すことはできない。　**135**

結婚式

kekkonshiki

Thank you for the invitation today.
本日はお招きいただき、ありがとうございます。
honjitsu wa omaneki itadaki arigatoo gozaimasu

Congratulations!
おめでとうございます。
omedetoo gozaimasu

I wish you all the best.
お幸せに！
oshiawaseni

The order of the ceremony（結婚式の流れ）

❶ Present a monetary gift and register→Take your seat.
受付で記帳して、お祝いを渡す→席に着く。

❷ Entrance→Speeches by the matchmaker and then by the main guests.
新郎新婦入場→仲人のスピーチや主賓の挨拶など。

❸ Make a toast and then start eating and drinking→Entertainments.
乾杯、食べ飲み始める→余興（よきょう）など。

❹ Seeing the guests off by the host families.
お見送り。

Seating Order (結婚式の席次)

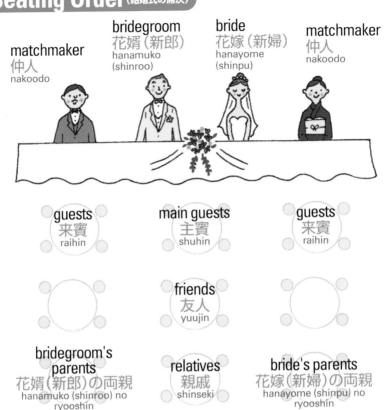

matchmaker
仲人
nakoodo

bridegroom
花婿（新郎）
hanamuko
(shinroo)

bride
花嫁（新婦）
hanayome
(shinpu)

matchmaker
仲人
nakoodo

guests
来賓
raihin

main guests
主賓
shuhin

guests
来賓
raihin

friends
友人
yuujin

bridegroom's parents
花婿（新郎）の両親
hanamuko (shinroo) no ryooshin

relatives
親戚
shinseki

bride's parents
花嫁（新婦）の両親
hanayome (shinpu) no ryooshin

PART6

Did you know? (知ってましたか?)

In Japan, we don't have a bridal shower, instead, the guests bring a monetary gift to the celebration. The monetary gift should be in a special envelope called "shuugi-bukuro" with ornaments.

●日本では、ブライダルシャワー（花嫁にプレゼントを贈るティーパーティ）はないので、招待客はお祝いに現金を持ってきます。現金は、"祝儀袋" と呼ばれるきれいな飾りのついた袋に入れます。

shuugi-bukuro（祝儀袋）→

葬　式
sooshiki

Attending a funeral (葬式に参列したら)

❶ register
記帳
kichoo

Register→Hand over your condolence money and write your name and address.
記帳→香典（こうでん）を渡し、名前と住所を書く。

❷ burn incense
焼香
shookoo

At first make a bow and hold the incense level with your forehead.
まず一礼。香（こう）をつまんで額の高さに。

Put the incense in the container. Repeat three times. Put hands together in prayer.
香を容器に入れ、これを3回くり返す。両手を合わせて祈る。

Make a bow to the family.
最後に親族に一礼。

❸ sacred purification rites
清めの塩
kiyome no shio

Sprinkle salt on the attendant before entering the house.
家に帰ったら、もらった塩をかけてお清めをする。

In Buddhism, a posthumous Buddhist name (kaimyoo) is given to the dead. (→和訳)

wake
お通夜
otsuya

funeral
告別式
kokubetsushiki

hearse
霊柩車
reikyuusha

crematory
火葬場
kasooba

funeral address
弔辞
chooji

condolatory telegram
弔電
chooden

condolence money
香典
kooden

return gift
お返し
okaeshi

In Japan, cremation is mandatory by law.
●日本では、法律で火葬が定められています。

Red and white are lucky colors, but black and white are not, that's why red and white are used for weddings and black and white are used for funerals.
●紅白はめでたい色、白黒は縁起が悪い色とされています。だから結婚式では紅白、葬式では白黒が使われるのです。

Did you know?（知ってましたか？）

When we see a hearse on the street, we make a fist putting the thumb inside. This is to protect our parents, as a "thumb" is referred to as "parents finger" in Japanese.

●霊柩車（れいきゅうしゃ）を見たときに親指をかくす人がいます。これは、自分の親を霊柩車から守るためです。日本語では"thumb"を"親(parent)指"と言うからです。

仏教では、死ぬと別の新しい名前が与えられる。これを戒名という。

日本の教育

nihon no kyooiku

School Activities（学校の行事）

commencement
卒業式
sotsugyooshiki

spring vacation
春休み
haruyasumi

entrance ceremony
入学式
nyuugakushiki

excursion
遠足
ensoku

the third term starts
3学期開始
san-gakki kaishi

school trips
修学旅行
shuugaku ryokoo

winter vacation
冬休み
huyuyasumi

midterm test
中間試験
chuukan shiken

summer vacation
夏休み
natsuyasumi

term-end test
期末試験
kimatsu shiken

sports day
運動会
undookai

camp school
林間学校
rinkan gakkoo

school festival
文化祭
bunkasai

concert
音楽会
ongakukai

the second term starts
2学期開始
ni-gakki kaishi

A schoolgirl asks the boy she likes for the second button of his uniform when they graduate.

Educational System（教育制度）

age **3~5**

kindergarten
幼稚園
yoochien

nursery school
保育園
hoikuen

age **6~12**

elementary school
小学校
shoogakkoo

age **12~15**

junior high school
中学校（中学）
chuugakkoo(chuugaku)

compulsory education
義務教育
gimukyooiku

age **15~18**

senior high school
高等学校（高校）
kootoogakkoo(kookoo)

age **18~**

university
大学
daigaku

junior college
短期大学（短大）
tankidaigaku(tandai)

graduate school
大学院
daigakuin

special training school
専修学校
senshuugakkoo

PART6

Did you know?（知ってましたか？）

Compulsory education attendance rate in Japan is almost 100%. About 95% of the children go to the high school and about 50% of them go to four-year universities or two-year junior colleges. Japan is one of the most educated countries in the world.

●日本では、義務教育にはほぼ100％就学、そして高校には約95％が進学、4年制の大学、あるいは2年制の短期大学には約50％が進学しています。世界で最も教育の盛んな国のひとつです。

美容と健康
biyoo to kenkoo

Hairdressing（理髪）

I'd like an appointment for two o'clock tomorrow.
明日の2時に予約したいのですが。
ashita no ni-ji ni yoyaku shitaino desuga

Haircut only, please.
カットだけお願いします。
katto dake onegai shimasu

Would you make it shorter?
短くしてください。
mijikaku site kudasai

Like this hairstyle, please.
こんな髪型でお願いします。
kon-na kamigata de onegai shimasu

hair salon	beautician	barbershop	baber
美容室	美容師	床屋	理容師
biyooshitsu	biyooshi	tokoya	riyooshi

perm	hair coloring	shampoo	shave
パーマ	ヘアカラー	シャンプー	ひげそり
paama	heakaraa	shampuu	higesori

Did you know?（知ってましたか？）

At the barbershop, if you don't specify haircut only, they will probably give you the full course, haircut, shampoo, and a shave.
●理髪店では、「ヘアーカットだけです」と言わないと、ヘアーカット、シャンプー、ひげそりのフルサービスになります。

haircut only

Most Japanese have little body odor. Perfume is not need to get rid of bad body odor.

Public bath (銭湯)

Let's go to the public bath.
銭湯に行きましょう。
sentoo ni ikimashoo

That sounds great.
おもしろそうですね。
omoshirosoo desune

Put your clothing in one of the free lockers.
- 服は無料ロッカーに入れる。

Wash and rinse yourself before you get in the bathtub.
- 湯船に入る前に体を洗い、よく流す。

draining floor
洗い場
araiba

bathtub
湯船
yubune

Be careful not to splash your neighbors.
- まわりの人にはねを飛ばさないように。

men's bath
男湯
otokoyu

women's bath
女湯
onnayu

attendant
番台
bandai

soap
石けん
sekken

hot water
お湯
oyu

cold water
水
mizu

plastic wash bowl
風呂おけ
huro-oke

hand towel
手ぬぐい
tenugui

During the Edo period, men and women bathed together in the public baths. They had barbershops and also tea and cookies were served there. It was a popular meeting place.
- 江戸時代の銭湯は、男女混浴でした。中には床屋があり、お茶や菓子なども出されて、一大社交場だったそうです。

PART6

毎日の天気
mainichi no tenki

Conversation（天気に関する会話）

What's the weather for tomorrow?
明日の天気は？
ashita no tenki wa

It'll be fine tomorrow.
明日は晴れです。
ashita wa hare desu

It's hot, isn't it?
暑いですね。
atsui desune

What's the temperature?
気温は何度くらいですか？
kion wa nando kurai desuka

It's over thirty degrees centigrade.
30度は超えています。
sanjuu-do wa koete imasu

It looks like rain, doesn't it?
ひと雨きそうですね。
hitoame kisoo desune

Typhoon No.10 is heading for Tokyo.
台風10号が東京に向かっています。
taihuu juu-goo ga tookyoo ni mukatte imasu

It's freezing	It's cool	It's warm	It's hot	It's burning
こごえそう	寒い	暖かい	暑い	すごく暑い
kogoesoo	samui	atatakai	atsui	sugoku atsui

Weather (天気や気温の表現)

 fine
晴れ
hare

 raining
雨
ame

 cloudy
曇り
kumori

 snowing
雪
yuki

 windy
風が強い
kaze ga tsuyoi

 hot
暑い
atsui

 cold
寒い
samui

 warm
暖かい
atatakai

 cool
涼しい
suzushii

 wet
蒸し暑い
mushiatsui

 burning
とても暑い
totemo atsui

 freezing
とても寒い
totemo samui

Temperature (温度)

In Japan, we use Centigrade instead of Fahrenheit. $F=\frac{9}{5}C+32$, 30℃=86°F.

● 日本では、温度は摂氏（C）を使っています。華氏（F）とは、$F=\frac{9}{5}C+32$で 30℃=86°Fとなります。

Did you know? (知ってましたか？)

When it rains, Japanese children make a "teruteru-boozu" (a paper doll they need to pray for fine weather).

● 雨が降ると、子どもたちは "テルテル坊主" を作って晴れるように祈ります。

日本人の好きなもの

nihon-jin no sukinamono

We have four definite seasons in Japan and according to the season we make a song and enjoy many events.
● 日本は四季がはっきりしているので、季節を楽しむために歌を作ったり、たくさんの行事をします。

Nature (自然)

桜 **cherry blossom**
sakura

In spring Japanese can't keep still when they think about cherry blossoms.
● 春になると、日本人は桜のことを考えて落ち着かないのです。

富士山 **Mt.Fuji**
hujisan

Japanese spiritual home.
● 日本人の心のふるさと。

茶摘み **picking tea**
chatsumi

The eighty-eighth day from the beginning of spring.
● 夏も近づく八十八夜。

田植えと稲刈り
taue to inekari **rice-planting & harvesting rice**

Rice planting is in early summer and harvesting rice is in autumn.
● 田植えは初夏、稲刈りは秋。

台風一過
taihuu ikka

beautiful weather after typhoon

A typhoon comes on the 210th day of spring=the lunar calendar.
- 立春から数えて、210日目ころに台風はやって来る。

雨 rain
ame

Even in the rain lovers enjoy walking under one umbrella.
- 雨が降っても、恋人同士は"あいあい傘"で楽しく歩きます。

満月 full moon
mangetsu

In old times Japanese imagined the figures on the moon as a rabbit pounding rice cake.
- 昔の日本人は、月の模様を"うさぎが餅つきをしている"と考えました。

PART6

風鈴 wind-bell
huurin

Feeling cool by the sound of the wind-bell.
- 風鈴の音で涼しさを感じます。

蓮 lotus
hasu

A lotus flower reminds Japanese Buddha.
- 蓮の花は、日本人にお釈迦様を思い出させます。

---

tering period.（→和訳）　　　4月になると、テレビで桜の開花予想を散るまでやる。

かぶと虫 **beetle**
kabutomushi

Kabuto means a samurai helmet. Mushi is an insect. Its head look like a samurai helmet.
●侍の兜に似ているのでこの名前がつきました。

こおろぎ **cricket**
koorogi

The chirping of a cricket is loved by japanese very much.
●日本人はこおろぎの鳴く声が好きです。

せみ **cicada**
semi

Any Japanese can tell you the names of a few types of cicadas.
●日本人ならだれでも、せみの種類を2〜3つは
知っています。

赤とんぼ **red dragonfly**
akatombo

> 夕焼けこやけの赤とんぼ〜
> yuuyake koyake no akatombo〜
> A red dragonfly in the sunset.

ちょうちょ **butterfly**
choocho

> ちょうちょ、ちょうちょ、菜の葉にとまれ〜
> choocho choocho nanoha ni tomare〜
> A butterfly stops by the rape blossoms.

からす **crow**
karasu

> からす、なぜ鳴くの？〜
> karasu naze nakuno〜
> Why does a crow caw?

Phrases（言葉）

立てば芍薬、座れば牡丹、歩く姿は百合の花
tateba shakuyaku suwareba botan arukusugata wa yurino hana

（美人の形容）

A beautiful woman looks like a peony when standing, a tree peony when sitting and a lily when walking.

梅にうぐいす、竹にすずめ
ume ni uguisu take ni suzume

（2つのものがよく調和していること）

The ume tree and the bush warbler always go together and so do the bamboo and the sparrow.

目に青葉、山、ほととぎす、初がつお
me ni aoba yama hototogisu hatsugatsuo

（初夏の季節感を視覚、聴覚、味覚でとらえた山口素堂の俳句）

Green leaves, a little cuckoo, and first bonito of the year.
Yamaguchi Sodoo

行雲流水
gyooun ryuusui

（物事に執着せず、自然〈流れる雲と水〉のままに行動すること）

We are free like a cloud in the sky and water in the stream.

体
karada

Parts of the body（体の各部名称）

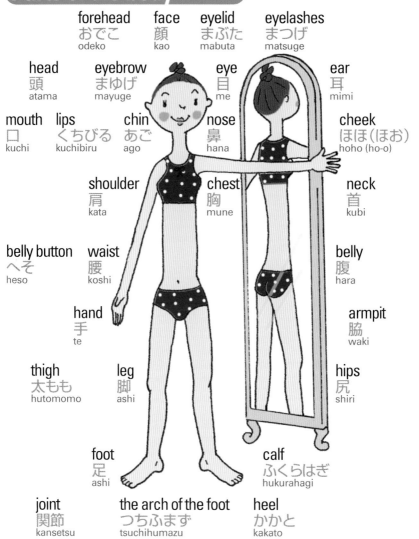

forehead
おでこ
odeko

face
顔
kao

eyelid
まぶた
mabuta

eyelashes
まつげ
matsuge

head
頭
atama

eyebrow
まゆげ
mayuge

eye
目
me

ear
耳
mimi

mouth
口
kuchi

lips
くちびる
kuchibiru

chin
あご
ago

nose
鼻
hana

cheek
ほほ（ほお）
hoho (ho-o)

shoulder
肩
kata

chest
胸
mune

neck
首
kubi

belly button
へそ
heso

waist
腰
koshi

belly
腹
hara

hand
手
te

armpit
脇
waki

thigh
太もも
hutomomo

leg
脚
ashi

hips
尻
shiri

foot
足
ashi

calf
ふくらはぎ
hukurahagi

joint
関節
kansetsu

the arch of the foot
つちふまず
tsuchihumazu

heel
かかと
kakato

The god of thunder will take your exposed belly button.(tradition)（→和訳）

Effective pressure points (つぼ)

Those points which are called "tsubo" are effctive for some symptoms.
- これらの "つぼ" と呼ばれるポイントを押したり、灸（きゅう）をすえると、いろいろな症状に効きます。

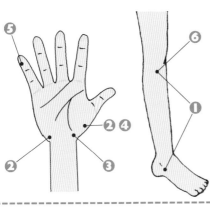

指　圧
shiatsu

finger pressure therapy

❶ lumbago
腰痛
yootsuu

❷ constipation
便秘
benpi

❸ stiff shoulders
肩こり
katakori

❹ diarrhea
下痢
geri

❺ headache
頭痛
zutsuu

❻ all diseases
万病
manbyoo

灸
kyuu

moxa cautery

Did you know? (知ってましたか？)

Japanese give a massage to their parents and grandparents especially on their shoulders. They call it "katamomi"(massage shoulders) or "katatataki"(pounding shoulders).
- 日本人は、よく両親や祖父母の肩をマッサージしてあげます。"肩もみ"、あるいは"肩たたき"と呼んでいます。

PART6

緊急事態

kinkyuujitai

To call police, dial 1-1-0.
警察を呼ぶときは、110番。
keisatsu wo yobutoki wa hyaku-too-ban

To call the fire engine and the ambulance, dial 1-1-9.
消防車、救急車を呼ぶときは119番。
shooboosha kyuukyuusha wo yobutoki wa
hyaku-juu-kyuu-ban

emergency button
Push the button and dial 110 or 119.
ボタンを押して110番か119番にかけます。

Help me!
助けて！
tasukete

Fire!
火事だ！
kaji da

Thief!
泥棒！
doroboo

Call~, please!
〜を呼んでください。
~ wo yonde kudasai

I forgot my bag at the station.
バッグを駅に忘れました。
baggu wo eki ni wasuremashita

Where is~?
〜はどこですか？
~ wa dokodesuka

I found my wallet.
財布は見つかりました。
saihu wa mitsukari mashita

policeman
警察官
keisatsukan

police
警察
keisatsu

hospital
病院
byooin

fire engine
消防車
shooboosha

ambulance
救急車
kyuukyuusha

Words（そのほかの単語）

traffic accident
交通事故
kootsuujiko

robbery
盗難
toonan

pickpocket
スリ
suri

molester
痴漢
chikan

stalker
ストーカー
sutookaa

snatch
ひったくり
hittakuri

threat
恐喝
kyookatsu

fraud
詐欺
sagi

shoplifting
万引き
manbiki

loss
紛失
hunsitsu

criminal
犯人
han-nin

arrest
逮捕
taiho

be lost
迷子
maigo

evacuation
避難
hinan

emergency exit
非常口
hijooguchi

homicide
殺人
satsujin

kidnapping
誘拐
yuukai

Hittakuri!

Did you know?（知ってましたか?）

From old times, Japanese people have been afraid of an earth-quake, a thunder, a fire, and a father in order("jishin-kaminari-kaji-oyaji"). But now it is said only a father isn't feared any more.

●昔から、日本では "地震、雷、火事、親父" がこわいものの代表でしたが、今、親父だけこわくなくなったと言われています。

oyaji

Earthquake (地震)

What you should do when you have an earthquake?
地震にあったらどうしたらいいか？

❶ Protect your head with an emergency hood, a cushion, a helmet, etc.
緊急用のずきんや座布団、ヘルメットなどで頭を守る。

❷ Go under the table and hold the legs of the table.
テーブルの下にもぐり、脚を押さえる。

❸ Open the door or window to escape.
ドアや窓を開けて、逃げ道を確保する。

❹ Put the fire out.
火を消す。

❺ Do not jump out of the house.
あわてて外へ飛び出さない。

Seismic Intensity (震度)

seismic intensity 1
震度 1

seismic intensity 2
震度 2

seismic intensity 3
震度 3 カタ カタ

seismic intensity 4
震度 4

seismic intensity 5
震度 5

seismic intensity 6
震度 6

INDEX

INDEX

INDEX

さくいん

さくいん

●著者

桑原功次（くわばら　こうじ）

慶応義塾大学経済学部卒。世界70余か国10万キロを走破、その体験を生かした英会話の教え方には定評がある。現在、グレイス英語スクール校長、グレイス・インターナショナル・コーポレーション代表取締役。
著書に『CD付き　英会話に役立つフレーズ100』『CD付きこれからはじめる英会話』『CD付き　はじめての英会話』『CD付き　絵で見る覚える英会話』『CD付き　はじめてでも困らないホームステイの英会話』（いずれもナツメ社）などがある。

〈グレイス英語スクール〉
〒110-0002
東京都台東区上野桜木2‐3‐2

■イラスト　高木一夫(Part1,2,3,4)、藤田ヒロコ(Part6)、和田慧子(Part2,5)
■撮　　影　金田邦男
■撮影協力　株式会社モンテローザ (http://www.monteroza.co.jp)
■編集協力　㈱文研ユニオン

書籍の最新情報はナツメ社ホームページをご覧ください。
http://www.natsume.co.jp

英語で紹介する日本

2006年9月30日発行

著　者　桑原功次　　　　　　　　　　©Kuwabara Koji, 2005
発行者　田村正隆

発行所　株式会社ナツメ社
　　　　東京都千代田区神田神保町1-52 加州ビル2F (〒101-0051)
　　　　電話　03(3291)1257(代表)　　FAX　03(3291)5761
　　　　振替　00130-1-58661

制　作　ナツメ出版企画株式会社
　　　　東京都千代田区神田神保町1-52 加州ビル3F (〒101-0051)
　　　　電話　03(3295)3921(代表)

印刷所　ラン印刷社

ISBN4-8163-3892-6　　　　　　　　　　　Printed in Japan